Pam Ayres has been a regular on television and radio since winning the talent show *Opportunity Knocks* in 1975 – featuring in *Just a Minute, The Comedy Quiz, Countdown* and her own series, *Ayres on the Air*. She performs her solo stage show throughout Britain and around the world and has a huge fan base in the UK, Australia and New Zealand. Pam is one of Britain's best-loved personalities and was awarded the MBE in 2004.

Also by Pam Ayres

BERTHA AND THE RACING PIGEON
GUESS WHO
GUESS WHAT
GUESS WHERE
GUESS WHY
WHEN DAD CUTS DOWN THE CHESTNUT TREE
WHEN DAD FILLS IN THE GARDEN POND
THE BEAR WHO WAS LEFT BEHIND
JACK CRATER
PIGGO AND THE NOSEBAG
PIGGO AND THE TRAIN RIDE
PIGGO AND THE FORK-LIFT TRUCK
SOME OF ME POEMS
SOME MORE OF ME POEMS
THOUGHTS OF A LATE-NIGHT KNITTER
THE BALLAD OF BILL SPINKS' BEDSTEAD
ALL PAM'S POEMS
DEAR MUM
THE WORKS
THE NUBBLER
WITH THESE HANDS
THE NECESSARY APTITUDE
YOU MADE ME LATE AGAIN
THE LAST HEDGEHOG

PAM AYRES

Surgically Enhanced

Illustrations by Susan Hellard

HODDER &
STOUGHTON

First published in Great Britain in 2006 by Hodder & Stoughton
An Hachette UK company

4

Copyright © Pam Ayres 2006

Illustrations © Susan Hellard

A CIP catalogue record for this title is
available from the British Library

Hardback ISBN 9781529378320
Paperback ISBN 9780340922798

Printed and bound in Great Britain by
Clays Ltd, Elcograf S.p.A.

Hodder & Stoughton policy is to use papers that are natural,
renewable and recyclable products and made from wood grown
in sustainable forests. The logging and manufacturing processes
are expected to conform to the environmental regulations
of the country of origin.

Hodder & Stoughton Ltd
Carmelite House
50 Victoria Embankment
London EC4Y 0DZ

www.hodder.co.uk

Contents

I'm Going to be Surgically Enhanced   1

Growing Up   4

They Should Have Asked My Husband   14

Reading the Map   18

Don't Kiss Me!   22

Learning French   24

I Want to go Home   29

Chamber of Horrors   32

The Pike in the Pub   34

The Downhill Skier   35

Call Out the Mountain Rescue!   48

Walking to Falkirk   51

Glasses   54

If I Only Had My Glasses, I'd Be There   55

Adopting a Dog   58

Bonemeal   66

A Place in the Sun   67

The Battle of Portaloo   70

The Nasty Cornish Pastie   74

Shopping on the Internet   75

There's Some Mistake   77

Job Applicant   79

Mixed Ward   83

The Packing Poem	84
Chorleywood	90
The Akaroa Cannon	93
At the Hairdresser	95
Hair, Proper Hair	98
MBE	100
Heart to Heart	101
The Young Lady of Dorking	104
Well Woman Check	105
Too Fat	108
Punch and Judy Man	111
The Pig Epistle	114
Wingit	117
Voice from the Doomed Dome	120
Automatic Telephone Answering Systems	123
Devastated	126
On the Panama Canal	128
Holiday Afloat	132
Inland Waterways	134
I Love a Little Narrow Boat	139
Global Warming	141
Woodland Burial	147
Crabby Christmas	148
Don't Bother, I'll Do It Myself	150
On White Horse Hill	152
Unfed Calf	154
Too Much of a Fag	156
Silver Wedding Speech	158
The Pension Poem	162
I Am Ready, Mr Prescott	165
Through the Lens	166

PAM
AYRES
Surgically Enhanced

I'm Going to be Surgically Enhanced

I stand before the mirror and I feel my spirits sink,
I'm so bored with this old body, it's so normal, round and
    pink,
It hasn't got the shingles or a heavy chesty cough,
But it needs a few adjustments; a few sections slicing off,
So jab it, stab it, use it, bruise it, give it all a tweak,
Insert the bags of saline in the hope that they don't leak,
Inject the collagen, carve me a monumental pout!
So I'll have lips of blubber once the stitches have come out.

I am going to have my neck done, it's so crêpy, slack and
    loose,
They haul it up and stretch, I think they do it with a noose.
I've been studying my bottom; it's not looking very well,
It needs lifting up and sculpting and judicious bags of gel,
So as I walk down the High Street and you view me from the
    back,
I'll be mischievous and bouncy like two ferrets in a sack,
And if I'm wearing Lycra you could have a heart attack,
For I'm going to be surgically enhanced.

Now I've got another problem, that I get the shakes at night,
I think it's the result of all the cheques I've had to write.
I am having liposuction on my abdomen and thighs,
I'm hoping to reduce myself to quarter of the size,
They use a kind of vacuum-cleaner needle, don't you know,
They stick it in your midriff and they drive it to and fro,
Slurp! And there's your problem in the bucket down below,
For I'm going to be surgically enhanced

I have felt decrepit lately but I suddenly feel better,
As I sniff the sweet aroma of the operating theatre,
So come on, Mister Surgeon, celebrate and pop the cork,
I'll lay on the table and you get your knife and fork.
I'm signing the indemnity and coughing up the cash,
Maybe I am profligate, extravagant and rash,
But I want a younger face! I don't care how they do it, dears,
I think they lift it up and kind of loop it round your ears.

Considering my bosom, well, it's looking rather sad,
But then I must remember that two children I have had,

And in my fond maternity produced a potent brew,
So now the kids are fifteen stone and over six feet two.
But returning to the bristols, I don't want the past to wreck
    them,
So I'm going to have them surgically enhanced like Mrs
    Beckham,
I can't afford the luxury and treatment that she can,
So I've booked in on the cheap to have it done in Pakistan.

My husband can regard himself a very lucky man
That I'm going to be surgically enhanced.

Growing Up

I was born in Stanford-in-the-Vale, in the Vale of the White Horse in Berkshire, and went to the village primary school with all the local children. Though we didn't necessarily like each other, we all knew each other and without realising it, were a small strand of what came to be known as the baby boomers, the great swathe of British children born during the same period after their dads came home from the war.

It's true to say that the surrounding countryside was our playground, and though hazardous it was very varied and thrilling. The focus used to shift from one excitement to the other. There was a thick knotted rope hanging from a tree branch over the brook near one of the mills. The bigger boys would seize the rope, pace backwards, then thunder up to the bank, swing over and let go at the precise moment which would enable them to soar out and land safely on the other side. The take-off bank was bald of grass, a bare runway for a succession of dusty, clapped-out shoes. I remember watching enviously, too small, scared and irrelevant to take part.

Those older boys were both dazzling and dangerous. They did spectacular things. They built a real tree house with a rope-ladder. They built an underground dugout with a chimney that smoked. They put sealed water-filled treacle tins into the heart of a bonfire until, to rousing cheers, the tin exploded and shot yards into the air. Each one of our days was different, with crazes that came and went. Though these included marbles, cricket, high jump, conkers, rounders, rabbiting and push-bike speedway, the actual list was boundless. It was also seasonal.

The River Ock, alive with water voles, ran through Stanford and made possible all manner of joyous activity. In the heat of summer we swam in it, in its winter flood we feared it, and all year we scavenged along it for delicious food.

There was a bend in the river called Big Ben, which was popular for swimming. The banks were thickly silted and sprouted a lush type of razor-sharp rushes. Nobody could afford water-wings, inflatable rings or blow-up crocodiles even if they had been available, so to ensure buoyancy we would uproot an armful of rushes and form them into a coarse ball. With flayed hands, this was placed beneath the skinny chest and would keep the doggy-paddler afloat for a limited time. The secret was to learn to swim before the rushes sank.

The River Ock was home to a multitude of fish, none of which were left undisturbed. Trout, roach and dace were regularly caught and so, spectacularly, were crayfish, a type of small olive-green freshwater crustacean shaped like a lobster. These were hunted with a trap fashioned from a bicycle wheel. Upon the hub of the wheel would be fixed a nugget of putrefying meat. Liver, giblets, anything that stank would do. Beneath the wheel would be secured a net so that nothing could fall through the spokes. Wires were attached around the rim of the wheel and extended up to the end of a long bean stick. This ramshackle device was then optimistically lowered into the sluggish waters of the Ock. Soon it would be yanked back up and in that astonishingly short time the trap would have attracted enormous numbers of crayfish. The Ock must have been seething with them. They would be heaped on the bicycle wheel, clinging vainly to the netting and to each other, unwisely in my opinion.

The trap would descend time and time again and the crayfish collected would be shaken into a sack.

When my mother saw the pulsating sack being borne up the village street she would leave the house. She was a kind person and found the scene that followed too merciless. Two tin baths usually hung on the back wall of our house. One was a very long bath for people and the other was an oval bath for washing clothes. This oval one would be selected, a bonfire was stoked up in the garden, water boiled up in the bath and the luckless crayfish dumped in. There would be a futile, desperate struggle to escape.

When they were cooked the crayfish turned red like the crabs and lobsters you see on fish counters. Then my mother would come home. Preparations would be made for the feast. Mum would cover the kitchen table with newspaper. There would be a large loaf of bread and a pat of butter. All eight members of the family would be armed with either a pair of pliers or a hammer, so it wasn't what you might call silver service. The crayfish would be tipped in a great clattering scarlet heap on to the middle of the table, and everybody would beat the living daylights out of them in order to extract the white, delicately flavoured and delicious meat. It was a fairly barbaric scene but the food was glorious and free, from the bounteous River Ock, provider too of watercress, moorhens' eggs, pike and eels.

Other delicious food followed on as the seasons progressed. We collected blackberries, glowing darkly in countless baskets and washing-up bowls. Mum made two things with them, blackberry and apple jam, and stewed blackberry and apple, and it was very difficult for the untutored eye to tell them apart because Mum's jam suffered from the irritating condition that it never set. If you wanted a jam sandwich you just poured some out on to the bread and paddled it about it bit. The sandwich would go maroon.

Once Mum made some rose-hip wine, reputed to be most beneficial and brim-full of vitamin C. Unfortunately it was also brim-full of little yellow hairs due to the limitations of the filtration process. It was a curious-looking wine: thick, salmon-pink and hairy.

From time to time, neighbours would have a glut of fruit and would pass round the surplus. Plums, damsons and greengages would appear and be preserved by bottling in the faintly unsettlingly named Kilner jars.

As the autumn came on we would go in search of mushrooms, that most mysterious of fungi which covers a field one year and deserts it for the next decade. Big, black-gilled, strong-flavoured mushrooms which we fried up with bacon and which exuded a dark meaty broth. You dabbled your bread in it and it turned black as coal.

Next came nuts. We collected sweet chestnuts and hazelnuts, swarming like monkeys up the trees. The sweet chestnuts we roasted over the fire on the coal shovel and our evenings were enlivened when they exploded, spattering the hearth and us with a creamy shrapnel. Horse chestnuts we knotted on strings as conkers. We swiped and struck and our hands were livid with bruises.

Bonfire Night was an important event and all the Vale villages vied with each other to produce the most impressive fire. Sometimes there was sabotage and a raiding party would go out and set fire to a neighbouring bonfire in October but this practice was rare and frowned upon.

I loved bonfire collecting. I used to pull dead and not-so-dead branches out of the hedgerows and drag them back along the car-free road to the bonfire. If you zigzagged from side to side, the branch made interesting patterns in the dust. Stanford was a stimulating place to live.

Though, as children, we did all we could to increase the size of the bonfire by adding shoe boxes, newspapers and suchlike, it wasn't until the last couple of nights before Bonfire Night itself that we saw how big our bonfire was eventually going to be.

This was because during these last two nights, under cover of darkness, men would creep out of our row of houses carrying repulsive old stained mattresses, and whirl them up on to the top of the bonfire. This had to be done during the dead of night because nobody wished to be identified as the owner of the mattress, or the person so lacking in fastidiousness that he might have slept on it. It was perfectly possible to look at one of these mattresses and trace the entire course of a somebody's life. You could see where somebody had been born; somebody had died; and all the human transactions in between.

Of this inexhaustible list of activities, my favourite was playing with hay bales during haymaking in June. Then all the small meadows that surrounded the village would be cut for hay. The bales would be stacked into towers ready to be taken back to the safety of the farmyards. Before the farmer had the chance to do that, however, a great horde of village kids, including myself, would turn up and rearrange the bales into much more interesting shapes.

Boys tended to make warlike structures, forts, castles and various kinds of platforms from which they could sling missiles at each other, but we girls set our sights lower and homelier. We built houses. Endless hay-bale houses, all of the same design with two bales end-to-end forming the sides, one bale across the top, built up and roofed with further bales and finally finished with an igloo-type tunnel entrance. When all was done, the builder would get down on to all fours and crawl into the bale house for an inspection. It would be dark, humid, suffocatingly hot and filled with the pungent aroma of newly mown hay. I used to spend *hours* in the bale houses. There were eight of us in our house so it was a great novelty to have a room of your own, even if it was only made out of grass.

However, your joy was usually short-lived because you were evicted by older kids, who had much more salacious intentions for the bale house. They wanted to go in for a snog. This caused great excitement among the others in the field because most of the families were related to each other. "Ere!' somebody would confide loudly, 'our Mary's in there with your Dave!' Then some wag would haul a bucket of water out of the brook and tip it in on top of them to cool their ardour. So you can see that my upbringing in Stanford was very racy indeed.

I think now, looking back, it was a very good thing that something racy was happening because at that time, during the fifties in rural Berkshire, certainly as far as I was concerned and I am convinced as far as most of my friends were concerned too, the teaching of the facts of life was very limited indeed. In fact, in all honesty, the only instruction I ever received on the subject was my mother wagging her finger at me and saying:

'Don't you go bringing any trouble back here!'

And that was about it. That was the beginning and the end of my sex education. When I think about it now, half of me wants to cackle with laughter and the other half wants to weep. It seems so daft now, that coyness, that reluctance to acknowledge the fact of reproduction. It was all brushed under the carpet. Pregnant women kept themselves out of sight and covered their shape in marquee-like garments with enormous bows at the throat. In our farming community, bulls, rams, boar pigs, billy-goats and cockerels copulated enthusiastically on all sides but to the adults I knew, it was all invisible. If you ever plucked up the courage to ask what was going on, adults said stupid, irritating things to you such as 'Well, if I told you *that*, you'd be as wise as I am!'

It was hardly surprising that you grew up with a weird attitude. Nobody ever sat me down and told me the facts; said something sensible like 'Now, you're growing up fast and you need to know, for your own protection and well-being, how things work between men and women.' Not a hope.

The way it was done was that you were presented with a series of indisputable facts. The first and most vital of these was this: that Men Were Only After One Thing. You didn't know what it was, but they were after it all right, and it was your solemn Christian duty to stop them from getting it. This was by no means as straightforward as you might think because it appeared that they would resort to subterfuge. Mum used to warn: 'They'll say anything. They'll say anything they think you want to hear, to get what they want.' She had a very high opinion of men.

You didn't just receive these warnings from your own mum, you would hear them from other people's mums as well. I got on very well with a lovely lady who lived just down the street from us. She was not unusual in that she had fourteen children. Many women in our village had huge families. I remember she was talking to me one day, giving me some advice I suppose, though I certainly didn't realise it. She said in this wistful way:

'Ah, don't you do what I did, Pammie. You get the ring on your finger first!'

I said, 'All right' and went home but really I didn't have a clue what she really meant. I wasn't very worldly. I was only interested in my bantams. Another thing my mum used to say which mystified me was this: 'It's the woman who has to carry the can!' I thought, 'What can? I don't know what you're *talking* about!' I thought she meant the paraffin can, we had one of those.

My best friend said that when her mother decided to broach the subject of sex to her it was a nightmare. She said, 'I didn't recognise my mother, she must have been psyching herself up in another part of the house and really, she was all of a twitch. What she actually managed to splutter out, in the heat of her embarrassment was: "I suppose, by now, you know the meaning of the word . . . connection." I thought she was talking about trains.'

That's how it was, and I think I would have remained in ignorance for a great deal longer had it not been for an incident on a local farm, when I saw something from which I learned a great deal in a very short period of time.

Like a lot of young girls I was mad about horses. There was no possible way we could afford one, but a family in the village kindly let me ride theirs. Their daughters had grown up and gone away to university and the pony was glad of the exercise. I used to ride him every Saturday morning and I looked forward to it all week. I daydreamed about riding along, seeing his mane and friendly pricked ears in front, hearing the lovely clippety-clop of his hooves.

One Saturday morning I went to catch him as usual. I had his bridle over my shoulder and an apple in my hand to tempt him. My way was down a farm track with an ivy-covered wall to my left. As I went along I became aware of a series of noises coming from the other side of the wall. I stopped and listened because they were noises such as I had never heard in my life. I could hear all this puffing and blowing, and grunting and gasping. I was intrigued and went over to have a look. (It's not going to be as bad as you think.)

Tucked up underneath the wall, in what I suppose she thought was a nice private spot until I loomed into view, was an enormous sow. She had detached herself from the other pigs in the field and made her way there. She was lying on her side and though I knew nothing about pigs, I could tell that there was something wrong. She was puffing and blowing, getting up, lying down and turning round agitatedly in small circles. Foam flecked the corners of her mouth. I was just about to run

back to the farm to fetch help when she lay down on her side with a final gasp. Her white eyelashes blinked, waiting. Then she slowly took in an enormous breath, bore down in a long groaning push, and a great line of piglets appeared at the other end. They were expelled with considerable force and lay wet and slithering on the grass. Suddenly they stirred into life and began to make their way to the front end where the sow greeted them with concerned and solicitous grunts. My jaw dropped a mile. Until that moment I had no idea that was how it worked; that something grew inside something else and was born. I remember looking down, marvelling at what I had just seen and thinking . . . 'Cor! That must have been where *I* came from!'

They Should Have Asked My Husband

I am of an age now when a lot of my friends' husbands are retiring. I notice that in some cases this is a triumphant success for the couple, whereas with others it takes a bit longer to get adjusted, particularly if he is a man of firm opinions.

This is about the person everybody's met who *knows it all*. It doesn't matter what your modest little view might be, he is going to *overwhelm* it with his great big, massively more important opinion.

I would like to point out that this has nothing at all to do with any member of my own family.

They Should Have Asked My Husband

You know, this world is complicated and imperfect and
    oppressed,
And it's not hard to feel timid, apprehensive and depressed,
It seems that all around us, tides of questions ebb and flow,
And people want solutions, but they don't know where to go.

Opinions abound but who is wrong and who is right?
People need a prophet, a diffuser of the light,
Someone they can turn to as the crises rage and swirl,
Someone with the remedy, the wisdom, the pearl . . .

Well, they should have asked my husband, he'd have told them
    then and there,
His thoughts on immigration, teenage mothers, Tony Blair,
The future of the monarchy, house prices in the South,
The wait for hip replacements, BSE and foot-and-mouth.

Yes, they should have asked my husband, he can sort out any
    mess,
He can rejuvenate the railways, he can cure the NHS,
So any little niggle, anything you want to know,
Just run it past my husband, wind him up and let him go.

Congestion on the motorways, free holidays for thugs,
The damage to the ozone layer, refugees, drugs,
These may defeat the brain of any politician bloke,
But present it to my husband, he will solve it at a stroke.

He'll clarify the situation, he will make it crystal clear,
You'll feel the glazing of your eyeballs and the bending of
     your ear,
Corruption at the top, he's an authority on that,
And the Mafia, Gaddafia and Yasser Arafat.

Upon these areas he brings his intellect to shine,
In a great compelling voice that's twice as loud as yours or
     mine,
I often wonder what it must be like to be so strong,
Infallible, articulate, self-confident and wrong.

Surgically Enhanced

When it comes to tolerance he hasn't got a lot,
Joy-riders should be guillotined and muggers should be shot,
The sound of his own voice becomes like music to his ears,
And he hasn't got an inkling that he's boring us to tears.

The Tony Blair soap opera is rolling on and on,
Is he staying? Is he leaving? Is he going? Has he gone?
And looking to the future, who is coming round the bend
But Gordon Brown, the laughing boy, the pensioner's best
    friend!*

My friends don't call so often, they have busy lives I know,
But it's not every day you want to hear a windbag suck and
    blow.
Encyclopaedias! On them we never have to call,
Why clutter up the bookshelf when my husband . . . knows it
    all.

* I update this verse constantly to keep it topical.

Reading the Map

My husband and I have been married for twenty-three years and for the most part, we get on very well. This was a pleasant surprise to me because to be honest I didn't go into the marriage with that much conviction. I thought, 'Well, I'll give it a try for a fortnight and see how I get on.'

As it turned out we get on fine, except for one thing. In just one area, we are guaranteed to fall out in a big way. I'm talking about long, venomous silences and the shooting of poisonous glances at defenceless backs. Sadly, the cause of these arguments is not something we can eradicate because it involves travel, and we travel all the time.

The problem arises when we are in our car, going somewhere we've never been before. My husband is driving the vehicle and

I have been given the task, which I didn't want, of reading the map.

When I was a single woman I had no trouble reading a map. I don't say I was better than anybody else but certainly I was no worse. I had my own little method. I would study the road atlas, make a list of the various towns and road numbers on the way to my destination, write them on a postcard, Blu-Tack it to the dashboard and mentally tick them off as I went along. It was a bit laborious but it never once let me down.

However, years of abuse, unfounded criticism and being told I've got the brain of a limpet, have sadly done two things. They have eroded my confidence. If all you hear for twenty years is someone mumbling under their breath, 'You're *useless*! You are *absolutely hopeless*!' then after a time you start to think, 'Well perhaps I am then. Perhaps I am.' With my confidence has gone my ability, and now I admit I'm not much good. I used to be able to do it but now I can't. I've lost it.

What rankles is that it's not my fault. It's his fault. He is like many men in that he is fortunate enough to have a kind of inbuilt sense of direction. It's marvellous. He seems to be able to divine where we are, and which way we need to go. Yet he'll never share it. He'll never say something generous like 'There's a difficult intersection up ahead, you might like to look at the map and brace yourself.'

I don't realise that something has gone wrong until I look up from whatever it was that I *shouldn't have been doing*, say reading a magazine or doing a crossword, and note firstly, that we are going round and round the inside lane of some terrifying great motorway roundabout, and secondly, that my husband is muttering something unintelligible to himself.

'Pardon?' I say in a chipper fashion. 'Pardon, I didn't catch what you said.'

Then I look at him and I realise that the reason I can't understand what he is saying is because he is actually talking to me through his teeth.

'Which way?' he is spluttering. 'Which *way* is it, you've got the ******* map!'

I look properly at him and get the shock of my life. His face has gone a repulsive beetroot red. You can feel the heat coming off him, like sitting next to a furnace. Peer at him closely enough and you can see the veins pulsating in his neck. He appears to be holding an invisible coconut in his right hand and is using it for emphasis as he shouts: 'Which way? WHICH WAY?'

Well, I challenge anybody to think straight in that intimidatory situation. With rising panic I look at the map. I can see the writing on it, but nothing comes in. For some reason our position on the map is always on the join, right down in the sewing.

'Which way?' he is still shouting. 'WHICH WAY?'

Well, I'm afraid I don't respond to being bullied. I say anything. I point to one of the roads and say, 'That one over there! Try that.'

He takes me at my word and we go off down that turning. Within a nanosecond we have both realised two things: one, that it is the wrong road, and two, that it is the longest road on the face of the Earth which has nowhere to turn round.

Now a ghastly but interesting change has come over my husband. All the heat has dissipated away and has been replaced by a cold, icy fury. He is rigid, stiff as a board. Gimlet-eyed, his mouth has changed into an obscene little button through which you can see his front teeth working, as he mouths silent obscenities. On down the long road we go, we happy couple.

Eventually, mercifully, we see a lay-by or a farm gateway in which we can finally turn round. Now I can tell you exactly the sequence of events which follows because I have seen it a fair few times. He indicates and crosses the road into the lay-by. Next he switches off the ignition and pulls on the handbrake. Now he performs an enormous, exaggerated, totally unnecessary sigh and while exhaling, shakes his head from side to side and assumes a strange frog-like smile in which there is no humour.

I hate that face. I would like a custard pie when he does that face.

His hand appears under my nostrils with the fingers doing little contemptuous flicking movements. It's for the map. He wants the map. Still talking to me through his teeth, he says in his long-suffering voice, 'Oh give it to ME!' I hand it over and I feel about half an inch tall, like a little chastised schoolgirl who has got it wrong yet again.

What consoles me about this story is that whenever I tell it to an audience, a large proportion of them seem to *recognise* the situation, as though there just might be other women in exactly the same boat . . .

Don't Kiss Me!

I want to ask a favour of the friends that I might meet,
To all of my acquaintances who pass me in the street,
Give me a cheery wave: 'Hello! How are you? Bye! So long!'
But don't kiss me. Please don't kiss me, for I always get it
    wrong.

I do not want to do it, I would rather pass you by,
I miss, you get a smacker on the ear or in the eye,
I'm standing on the pavement thinking 'Blast! Damnation!
    Heck!
He went the other way and I have kissed him on the neck.'

Surgically Enhanced

I find it so embarrassing, it makes my knuckles clench,
It's a very dodgy habit we've imported from the French,
What's wrong with 'Oh good morning!' or a handshake if you
 must,
A lovely smile of welcome or, all right, a smile of lust.

But I do not want to kiss you! I am sure you're very nice,
But I find it so confusing, is it once or is it twice?
I'm filled with apprehension, and a feeling close to fright,
Who leans forward first? Is it the left cheek first or right?

And I feel a strange awareness as we stand around and speak,
That there's a disconcerting trace of your saliva on my cheek.
So don't kiss me, no, don't kiss me, say *'Enchanté! Ciao!*
 Good health!'
But I'm telling you, don't kiss me, keep your choppers to
 yourself!

Oh don't kiss me, I implore you, for I cannot stand the strain,
I seldom kiss my husband and you don't hear him complain,
So *au revoir! Auf Wiedersehen!* Just tell me that you'll miss
 me
But *please,* if we should meet again, don't pucker up! DON'T
 KISS ME!

Learning French

I was invited to Antibes in the South of France to perform my one woman show in the little theatre there. It's very small and all done out in red plush. The only thing you have to try to put out of your mind as you walk on the stage in the hope of making people laugh, is that at one time it was a Chapel of Rest. This can have a dampening effect on your spirits.

My husband and two sons were also invited. The idea was that I would do the show for two nights and then we'd stay on for a week's holiday in the sunshine. It was a lovely invitation and I particularly wanted it to be a good, successful holiday because at the end of it, our two boys were going off on their gap-year trips to Australia, New Zealand and Hong Kong. It was our last family holiday together before we were all scattered.

I am reasonably happy with myself now. I think when you're younger you agonise about yourself, you'd like to change this and that, but now I'm all right. I quite like myself. The only thing I feel embarrassed about is that I don't speak any other languages. We never did any at Faringdon Secondary Modern School and afterwards I suppose I just never had the gumption to do anything about it.

In my normal life I don't think about it much, but occasionally my husband goes to France on business and I like to go with him. It's then that I feel so awful. Not knowing the language I can't participate. I have attended so many social gatherings with my husband in France and all you can do is to try to look amiable. You smile and nod, like a nodding dog in the back of somebody's car window. It's deadly and the evening seems endless.

I didn't want it to be like that for our family holiday. Just for once I didn't want to be the duffer at the back who can't even ask for a cup of tea, the one whose constant cry is 'What did he say?' I thought, 'I know it's late in the day, but I'm going to try to learn a bit of French. Just a few basic things would help. It can't be that difficult surely, after all I've got 120 words per minute Pitman's shorthand! I can understand all those squiggles! Yes! I'll take the bull by the horns and go for it!'

I've got a computer at home. A lot of people think I write with a quill, but no, I've got a computer so I went down to the big computer emporium in Bristol to find an appropriate course. I chose one especially for Adult Beginners and it cost seventy pounds, so it wasn't cheap.

At home I prepared to get started, but I was surprised to find that I was nervous. When I analysed this feeling it was because it's one thing to fear that you've left it too late, that you're now too long in the tooth to pick up a new skill, but it's another thing to have it confirmed. Anyway I mustered up my courage and got cracking.

The whole thing was in French. That is to say, nothing was explained to you in English at all. A picture came up on the screen and a Frenchman with a nice kind supportive voice told you what it depicted. After that, a series of sentences appeared and you had to click on the phrase you had just heard. Having done that correctly you could go on to the next picture. It was a pleasant, straightforward method.

The first picture that came up on the screen was of a bird. A gull. You were looking up at it as it wheeled and turned in the sky. '*L'oiseau vole*,' the Frenchman declared in his friendly voice:

the bird flies. I shall never forget that. I've got it ready whenever I need it. You then clicked on the right phrase, and went on to the next picture.

This was of a fish. A large fish swimming along underneath the lily-pads. The Frenchman said, '*Le poisson nage.*' The fish swims. Well, I was mightily encouraged. I did not find it hard to retain these phrases at all. Indeed, it wasn't long before I found I could drop little witty fragments of French into the household conversation. I put the fish and chips on the table. 'There you are,' I said, '*Le poisson* don't *nage* any more! Wrap yourself round that lot!'

The family were impressed. Well, they went quiet anyway. Naturally my computer course couldn't keep teaching me things like here's a bird, here's a fish, we needed to move on. Now it adopted a slightly different approach. Little scenes were portrayed and the man described them. The first one was a walled vegetable garden in which there were two young men, two youths. One was throwing a garden rake to the other. Apparently this is a very popular pastime in France. '*Le garçon attrape le râteau!*' exclaimed the Frenchman, which means 'The boy catches the rake!'

I found myself absolutely hooked on the course and I worked until really late at night. It didn't overwhelm you but moved forward in encouraging little increments, so you'd think, 'Well, I got that right, I'll just see if I can get the next bit.'

Towards the end of the course it became much more difficult because conversations began to be included. The nice French man was still in his position on one side of the screen but now they introduced someone else. A woman. I didn't take to her. I preferred it when I had him to myself.

She had a sickly-sweet voice. A cloying, saccharine sort of voice. She appeared on the other side of the screen and between them now materialised a car. *La voiture*. The car. The lady asked a question of the man concerning it: '*Est-ce que la voiture est rouge?*' Is it that the car is red? Is the car red? Whereupon the Frenchman replied, '*Non! La voiture est bleu!*' No, it's blue. At this point the lady, who obviously had defective eyesight, then asked, '*Est-ce que la voiture est jaune?*' Is it yellow, as in jaundice?

Anyway, you get the idea.

This computer course had twenty-eight levels of skill and I worked my way through them all. At the end there was a random test when they fired questions at you from all the previous levels and I hope you will not think I am immodest if I tell you the truth, that I got a hundred per cent every time. I just cannot tell you what this did for my ego. Me, who had been afraid even to put the disk into the computer in case I couldn't do it.

You'll understand that now, when I thought about our forthcoming French family holiday, my feelings were transformed. Now, I thought, I'll be able to join in, chat, ask questions, pay

compliments, even make little jokes. At last I'll be a part of things. I could not wait.

You know what I'm going to say. I was disappointed. Bitterly disappointed on two counts. The first was that nowhere, in the length and breadth of France, did I meet anybody who spoke to me remotely like the nice man on the computer. Anyone who deigned to address me did so at the most amazing, phenomenal speed, like a Kalashnikov. The words of the man on the course were all divided up: there was a word then a space, a word then a space. I could follow it. Real French people spoke in a continuous ribbon of sound; you didn't know if the bit in the middle went with the bit before, or the bit that came afterwards. I gaped. I stood in Antibes market with all manner of business transactions going on around me and though I strained my ears I could not make out a single thing that I understood. I was mortified.

I was also disappointed by the infrequency with which I was called upon to use those phrases that I had so painstakingly learned. Nobody asked me to catch a rake. Everybody seemed to know what colour their car was. I returned from the holiday convinced that the entire computer course had been a total waste of time. However, I was wrong in my assumption. After a period I realised I was having small insights which I could not have had before. I'll give you an example:

At home we have cattle. During the winter I go out in the mornings and put hay into their manger. One morning I was doing this and I suddenly thought: 'Wait a minute . . . I bet the fact that this is called a manger is not unconnected with the fact that the French word for eat is *manger*! Yes!

Whether this was worth seventy quid, I remain to be convinced.

I Want to go Home

She intones a welcome, Miss glossy and hard,
And glances across me when swiping my card.
I lift up my eyes and digest what I see:
The conference delegates, tourists and me,
Security persons alert at the back
For bombers and hookers and dealers in crack.

She summons a porter, reluctant to shift,
She hands him a key and we walk to the lift.
He unlocks a room and he turns on the light
In another sad box for another sad night.
He shows me the minibar, TV and tray,
I show him a tip and he goes on his way.

I put down the bag and I sit on the bed,
The colours are desperate, cheerless and dead,
A shortage of light, an excess of heat,
A shower tray worn by anonymous feet,
Next door's television is loud in my ears,
My face is composed but my heart is in tears.

I'm nothing and no one to anyone here,
I could vaporise, levitate, flip, disappear,
I'm only a payment to keep to the path,
So I don't hang myself or get drowned in the bath,
No trashing of fittings or flinging of bread,
And no randy footballers busting the bed.

I'm just a debit card walking, that's all,
Of no consequence, something transient, small,
A mere overnighter, who washes, who eats,
Who necessitates somebody changing the sheets,
A pilferer maybe, who watches and prowls,
And might be inclined to make off with the towels.

At hotels and motels, in each B&B,
I don't want to know them; they don't want to know me.
To live from a suitcase? No, not any more,
With its lid opened back and its guts on the floor,
Where I hear in my heart like a sad metronome:
I don't want to be here. I want to go home.

Home. That collection so pitifully small,
With hardly a second-hand value at all,
What price this old table? This sofa and stool?
This masterpiece drawn by an infant at school?
Small treasures on shelving untidily shoved,
From places I went to with people I loved.

Home, where the clutter was chosen by me,
A log on the fire, a dog on the settee,
Where they know all about me, the good and the bad,
There's nothing to hide and nothing to add,
I am *dying* to be there, and in little doubt
That it's time to pack up. And it's time to check out.

Chamber of Horrors

Pam and Gordon are a middle-aged married couple. They have just come home from having a day out:

PAM: Well, I wish we hadn't gone.

GORDON: What, to the Tower of London? Why?

PAM: I thought it was disgusting, down in those dungeons, that hateful torture chamber, all those barbaric devices. And those *people*, salivating over it, taking in every detail, it was *revolting*. And I have to say you were one of them!

GORDON: Oh, let's get the supper and forget about it. Pass me that garlic.

PAM: What for?

GORDON: I'm going to crush it. And don't think you can protect that carton of cream.

PAM: Why?

GORDON: Because it's going to get a darn good whipping. Where have you hidden the black peppercorns?

PAM: What do you want them for?

GORDON: Because I'm going to crack them. I'll make them talk . . . I'll crack them if it takes me all day . . .

PAM: Gordon . . .

GORDON: These eggs . . . I'll beat them within an inch of their lives . . . and that bread . . . it's been holding out against me but I'll break it, you'll see, I'll break it in the end . . . and as for those tomatoes, well, I've got *plans* for them as well.

PAM: Gordon, why don't you sit down . . .?

GORDON: Yes, I'm going to drop them in boiling water and skin 'em! And that big baking potato, it's not too big for me! I'm going to stab it and gouge its eyes out! (*maniacal laugh.*) And see those onions, I'll make them sweat! Where's the cleaver?

PAM: No, I'm not doing this with you any more. I think the balance of your mind has been disturbed. I don't want what you're cooking, I'm going out to get some fish and chips.

GORDON: Fish eh?

PAM (*nervously*): Yes.

GORDON: Well just make sure they give it a darn good BATTERING.

The Pike in the Pub

A pike patrolled this waterway, intent upon predation,
His appetite unparalleled in this or any nation,
Until a roving fisherman with courage, skill and class,
Installed him, fellow drinkers, safe within these walls of glass.

The Downhill Skier

During my schooldays at Stanford-in-the-Vale Primary and Faringdon Secondary Modern, I went on two school trips. One was to the Ideal Home Exhibition in London and the other was to Buscot Water Works. At the Ideal Home Exhibition I remember being ecstatic over a free gift of sweet thick hand cream, and at Buscot Water Works we shuffled in cold conditions from one rectangular water tank to another, admiring fluff-like bits of alum. These, we were told, clung to impurities in the water, thus swelling their size and ensuring their entrapment in various filters. Sadly I have never found a use for this piece of information.

Everyone wants better for their children than they had themselves so when we had two small sons at school and interesting French ski trips came up, we were quick to hand over the money and fondly wave them off on the bus. In time they became adept skiers and the school ski trip a regular event.

Years passed and our eldest son left that school and went on to the next, where a ski trip was also on offer. However, having only just started there he didn't know anyone so was reluctant to go. Back at the first school the youngest son didn't want to go on their trip either because his brother wasn't going.

In due course I was approached by a small, hopeful delegation. Would *I* take them skiing? It seemed a laughable notion at first. *Me?* I was in my fifties and had never skied.

'Come on, boys,' I said. 'Ask me for something realistic. How can I take you skiing? I'm fifty-plus, have never skied in my life, can't speak the language and Dad won't come.'

Then my youngest son, James, said something that seemed immensely poignant to me. He said, 'We'll look after you, Mum.'

My heart melted. All the years I'd looked after them and now these two small boys had no doubt that they were going to look after me. For the first time, I thought more seriously about the proposition.

I remembered reading an article by Bernard Levin who discovered skiing at an advanced age, loved it and never looked back. I questioned myself: 'Right, I am fifty years old. Am I now going to call it a day? Am I never going to accept a new challenge? Just give up and coast into a decline? Is that what I want? At *fifty*! NO WAY! I'm fit, everything works, here are my two cracking sons wanting my company. I have the opportunity to do something brand new with the people I love most in the world. I'll GO FOR IT!'

We marched into the Cirencester travel agent and booked up a week in the French Alps in March. I told my husband about the bold plan and he fought to keep a straight face.

As the departure date raced towards us, I decided to investigate ski-wear and frightened myself by going into a smart shop in Cheltenham. Chastened by the ludicrous prices I made instead for C&A. They were still in business then, and had been a good source of ski-wear for the boys. I was looking for something cheap for me which would do the job for a week. After all, I thought, I may never go again. Sure enough I found a good jacket. It was red and a bit flash, with a multitude of flaps, zips and toggles. It had slogans down the sleeves. Down one arm was emblazoned the word 'GO!' and down the other 'ZOOM!' Several lengths of string with knotted ends swung from the garment and when I wore it to feed the chickens they jumped up and pecked at the knots.

Armed with a lengthy list from a previous school trip, I also bought salopettes, those padded trousers with straps over the shoulders, padded gloves, a bobble hat, two sets of neck-to-ankle thermal underwear in black, thick socks and a pair of cheap orange goggles. I did not see how the cold could get through that lot.

At that time I was having trouble with my knee and I went to see a specialist. Did he think, I asked him, that I would be unwise to try skiing in view of the fact that I was having these problems? He rolled my knee this way and that like a suet duff and said it seemed fine. I felt a sense of reassurance which evaporated seconds later when he laughingly warned, 'But you should try not to come back like one chap I saw recently. He had a skiing accident and managed to drive the ski pole *right through the calf of his leg*! Ha ha!' chortled the great man, 'he was well and truly kebabbed!'

I smiled a tight smile.

The day arrived and my husband took us to the airport. I could tell that he thought I was nuts. The flight was delayed by three and a half hours and for consolation we were given a voucher for three pounds to buy a sumptuous repast. At last the aircraft was ready for boarding and we hurried along the wide glassy concourse to the departure lounge. We were laughing and eager, the three of us, until I saw two people making slow progress towards us. A male nurse was pushing a woman in a wheelchair. She was about my age. Her leg was held straight out in front of her in a huge padded splint, encased in blue foam and held up with pulleys. As we passed each other she stretched the yellow skin of her face into a feeble smile. I smiled weakly back. I wanted to get her by the lapels of her nightie and demand, 'Did you do that skiing?' but in my heart I did not want to hear her answer.

We landed in Lyons in bright sunshine and were directed to one of the scores of lined-up coaches. It was hot. I sat with my two boys and now felt a lot less confident. A large horse-like woman got on the bus, with a party of twelve. I know this because she brayed in a loud posh voice, 'We're twelve. Shall we sit hyah?'

We left that bus at Moutier and were decanted into a minibus. The driver was leaning sullenly out of his window, sucking hard on a white-hot cigarette. Seeing our collection of suitcases he curled his lip, jerked his head violently backwards and muttered, '*Baggage* . . .' In other words, do it yourself. We heaved the bags on board and the minibus set off, winding up hairpin bends on the way to the various resorts. We passed ruined-looking old chalets. I half expected to see a ruined-looking old Julie Andrews totter out in a pinafore. The boys began to be alarmed about the snow because there wasn't any. Grey dead grass and the occasional hellebore stretched away over the slopes. We were travelling upwards but I felt a marked sinking of the spirits. At last, in gathering darkness we were dropped in a hotel car park and told to wait. Around us on the tarmac were a few thawing rolls of dirty snow. Nobody came.

Dragging our cases, we found our way to the squalid back door of the hotel to be told that not only were the boys and I not close to each other, we were on different floors. To my sons' horror and shame, I burst into tears. My room was a tiny basement cell in which hovered a sweet, vile stench of sewage and cabbage. My request for a change of room was dismissed with contempt. The 'ôtel, I was assured, was fully booked. I was tired and missing the loud, booming authority of my husband more than I could say. He would have got me out of that foul room in a minute.

That night in the restaurant it was *raclette*, which all the other diners seemed to understand involved melting cheese in a tiny battered pan. Other residents were in great happy parties. I could not inject any sense of fun, and began to wonder if one apprehensive middle-aged mother and two teenage boys was a recipe for success after all. I went to bed in my dismal room miles from the boys and felt nervous. I could hear the distant drone of piste bashers, the great bulldozers that smooth the snow. Their eerie headlights pierced the darkness like monsters circling each other far up on the mountains.

Things got worse. I woke up in the morning with a foul migrainous headache. At breakfast we choked on our croissants as we realised that the clocks had gone forward by an hour and at that precise time we were supposed to be outside the ski school waiting for our various instructors. Hot, hungry and in a frenzied rush we collected our hired equipment.

Ski boots, for anyone not fortunate enough to have tried

them, enclose the foot and ankle with the ferocity of a rat trap. Great levers have to be snapped shut to secure them. On standing up, you find that your weight is thrown curiously forward and you are forced to walk on tiptoe with the knees bent. At any moment, you think, you may suddenly fall down and pray. In my case this wasn't too far from the truth.

To be a successful skier you need to have tremendous strength and a very good memory. The boots you wear are very heavy. The skis are also heavy. Long and awkward, they are carried over the shoulder for much of the time and chafe all bony protuberances. Two ski poles must also be carried. Sunglasses or goggles are a must. They are not a vanity item but are essential to protect the eyes from the harmful rays bouncing up from the snow and which otherwise fry the eyeballs. More on this later. You need gloves. One day I forgot and the instructor warned: 'Wear your gloves! In case someone skis over your fingers. You will not be cut so bad.'

Next you need to remember a hat. Ninety-nine per cent of body heat, I was constantly reminded, is lost through the head. I had a white one with a mischievous pom-pom, only I didn't feel mischievous. Sun cream is required to protect all parts of the face, particularly the nose, and finally you need to remember your lift pass, a laminated photo of yourself enclosed within a plastic holder and worn on the arm like a tourniquet. Forget your lift pass at your peril because without it you may be marooned up a glacier, unable to return to your hotel.

Equipped and heavy-laden, we were ready to start the first day. My sons were claimed by the holiday company rep, who was also a ski guide. She told them about the various entertainments organised for the week: a quiz night (later cancelled due to lack of support), and a hot rocks night where you are given a hot rock on which to cook your food. She also said, 'Honestly, boys, I think your mother is so brave to start skiing *at her age.*'

I was troubled to hear this, as I had not realised I would be such a rarity. Then they glided smoothly away with beautiful alternate strokes to be shown the good runs, the best lifts, and to be given a general picture of the area.

After they had gone I took up my position on the forecourt of a large chalet housing the ski school. It looked a bit like a bus station. Queues had formed beneath lollipop signs bearing descriptions. I stood, with a few others, beneath one which said *Adulte Débutante*. Adult Beginner. The sun blazed down. It was as hot as the fires of hell. I was wearing all my gear, including the black neck-to-toe thermal underwear, and thinking of everybody I had ever heard of who'd spontaneously combusted.

At 9.30 a.m. an expectant hush fell over the queues as the chalet doors opened and the ski instructors filed out. They looked impressive. Each one was dressed in a fiery red ski suit with a jagged blue mountain-range symbol on the chest. Each wore sunglasses with mirror lenses and had floppy gleaming hair, white teeth and the graceful movement of the supremely fit. They beckoned their fawning queues and skied away.

Except for our instructor. Ours looked like a bald Ronnie Corbett. He walked with a gnome-like, toddling gait, the red suit unflatteringly tight about his bottom. I remembered an old phrase of my dad's: two apples in a paper bag. The instructor's name was Philippe and we did not take to each other.

A hateful process of humiliation followed. Even now, years later, recalling it makes me cringe.

He lined us up. 'Ski towards me on one ski only!' he ordered. I was only one stage on from skiing on all fours. I couldn't do it. I dared not lift the second foot.

'What's wrong with you, Big One?' he jeered. 'You got chewing gum stuck under your ski?'

Everybody laughed.

41

He began to talk to us about the proposed programme for the week. Though he was already a small man it seemed to me that he was becoming smaller. Too late I realised that this was because we were standing on ground which slightly sloped away. I was sliding backwards on my skis without a clue what to do about it. Aghast, I glided silently down the snowy slope and fell over. Philippe watched from the top as I struggled to get up. It is nearly impossible to stand up from a prone position while wearing skis. It is like having shoes fifteen feet long. They slide out from under you. You flounder and thrash trying to get them to face the same way. You rise halfway up and fall back. You are humiliated and look an utter fool.

With a pained sigh Philippe came down to where I was and contemptuously stood on my ski so that I could stand.

'You, Big One,' he murmured nastily, 'you are holding up ze whole group. Maybe you should join a different class.'

By now my migraine headache was full blown. I walked back to the hotel and threw up all day in the stinking cell. Through the window I watched thawing snow drip off the roof, and listened to the happy chatter of families lunching on the wide veranda of the hotel. One mother with ringing tones and particularly cut-glass speech was on a mobile phone to her Hampshire butcher. I listened sourly to what she said.

'It's Juliet! I'm in the French Alps! Oh, the weather's glorious! Oh, it's glorious there too? Oh fentestic! Now Jack, I want you to send me up a nice piece of sirloin on Saturday, for eight. Will you do thet? Oh thenk you so much! Ah well, beck to the sweat!'

That evening the boys were dejected to come back and find their mother grey and prostrate, unlike the other jolly mothers. My eldest son had the white shape of his goggles clearly visible against the pink skin of his face. I commented on this and he explained that he had forgotten to put on any sunscreen.

Next day I felt shaky but better and went out to join the group to which I had been relegated. When I saw the people waiting in this queue I thought of my father.

Dad was ill for about eighteen months before he died. Gradually his great strength and energy diminished to nothing. While he still could, he used to drive Mum to White Horse Hill on the Berkshire Downs, above the village of his birth, Uffington. It was dear and familiar to him and he loved the panorama of villages spread out below. White Horse Hill has gradually become a controlled place with signage, regulations and designated car parking. The official car park is now a very long walk from the top of the hill. One day they'd been up there, and I asked Dad how he coped with this walk from the main car park.

'Oh, we never parks there,' he explained, 'we parks in the one near the top, the Pensioners and Cripples.'

'You can't say that any more, Dad,' I told him. 'You have to say Senior Citizens and the disabled.'

'Ah,' he nodded, 'I be too old to change now my gal. It'll always be Pensioners and Cripples to I.'

So when I saw the group of skiing hopefuls I was now to be a part of, my father's old non-PC phrase came back to me. Nothing more aptly described the timid little straggle. I joined the rock-bottom class, the no-hopers. I joined the Pensioners and Cripples.

A goddess appeared in a gold leather baseball cap. Through the hole at the back was threaded a thick flaxen pony-tail. This was our instructor, Sandrine. A saviour. She was just what I needed, and as kind as Philippe was poisonous. 'Put on your skis!' she called in a happy bell-like voice. '*On-y-va!* Off we go!'

She weaved among us in her gold hat, skis singing, graceful as a dancer. We hesitantly shuffled off. She kept up a constant sweet stream of encouraging exhortations: 'Don't twist your body! Put your weight on your downhill ski! Stand up straight! Release your upper leg! Relax! Relax! Bend your knees!' To me she urged, 'Smile, Pom, you are on 'ollyday!' I followed behind, face contorted with concentration under the woolly hat.

Through ignorance I had booked our holiday much too late in the season. The snow had receded far from the village, so we had to travel long distances to the remaining hard, icy slopes. We were conveyed there by differing designs of ski-lift and upon arrival, I fell off every one. The beauty of the enormous vistas was lost on me because I couldn't see how I was going to negotiate them to get back to the hotel. This skiing was much too advanced for me. I was terrified and doing mental deals with God: 'If you'll only get me off this mountain I'll be different . . .'

One day we had to traverse across the top of a steep slope. I could not hold the snowplough position and I fell far down, over and over. At last I stopped rolling and lay spread-eagled. Sandrine whisked up beside me: 'Your knees, Pom! Are your knees all right?' My knees survived but a vast, interesting bruise developed on my leg in the shape of various coins, a chapstick and the key to my hotel room. That night my husband rang to see how we were getting on. 'Oh,' they told him, 'Mum went over a cliff.'

Over the next couple of days I did make faltering progress with Sandrine. She was nice. I began to think the worst was over but no, it wasn't.

I did not like the look of the sunburn on my son's face. The area unprotected by goggles or sun cream had turned a dull red. Yellow watery blisters had started to form on his cheeks. It looked ominous and it hurt.

One evening we were famished and ate this meal placed before us: a twisted heap of spaghetti, broccoli florets, a flaked almond and a great slab of black meat. When I looked at it I thought I could hear a ghostly whinny. That night my sons and half the hotel went down with food poisoning. They were dismally ill. In the mean room I could do none of the nice comforting things I could have done for them at home and I felt desperate. Additionally, the sunburn had turned into vile watery bags. I skied inexpertly down to a nearby village where there was a pharmacist. I propped my skis up outside the door and went in. I knew exactly what I wanted to say: 'Good afternoon,' I would begin, 'I have two sons, both suffering from a particularly virulent form of stomach upset. They have repeatedly vomited and look pale and exhausted. In addition, my elder son has severe sunburn on his face, with great watery blisters, and is in considerable pain. I wonder if you could recommend some suitable medication for both conditions from your comprehensively stocked shelves. Money is no object. Thank you.'

That is what I would have liked to say. Having no grasp of French beyond 'Two cups of coffee and a beer', however, I was reduced to the most primitive sign language. The pharmacist watched with alarm as I stuck my fingers down my throat and mimed the yellow blisters and blazing sun. I left laden with expensive preparations all meticulously labelled in French I couldn't read.

By the end of the week my sons began to feel better and did a little skiing but we'd had enough and were longing to go home. On the morning of our departure I awoke to find that I now had the bug and was in the grip of the most violent sickness. My sons packed and carried my suitcase and thus began the worst journey of my life, travelling home all day across France.

Later, I wrote the following poem as a farewell to skiing.

Downhill Skier

For sale:
One goggle with elastic round the ears,
Stained with perspiration and with tears,
One photo of beginners' class, grouped,
And one bobble hat – drooped.

Photographs of mountains and of snow,
Of people that I didn't get to know,
Me laughing in the snow and waving mitt,
Pretending to be glad. A hypocrite.

Surgically Enhanced

One salopette, elasticated calf,
One cartilage in kneecap, torn in half,
One book of useful phrases learned for days,
And ridiculed by Frenchmen in cafés,

One lift map showing type: drag, T-bar, chair,
With length of queue anticipated there,
In agonising detail I recall,
How surely I fell screaming from them all.

One postcard showing icy mountain range,
One bruise, the shape of hotel key and change,
Tears of humiliation hotly dabbed,
And voodoo doll of ski instructor, stabbed.

For sale, one skiing jacket, hardly worn,
Suitable for up the Matterhorn,
Excellent condition, perfect fit,
Retirement sale. Owner forced to quit.

Call Out the Mountain Rescue!

While making a series for BBC Radio, I spent an energetic day with the Mountain Rescue Team at Ambleside in the Lake District. It was interesting to hear about the different situations the team attends, and I was impressed by their wide-ranging skills and quiet willingness to go out in hostile conditions to help others.

On their behalf, I was indignant that people waste their time and ignore warnings. Visitors totter off into the hills in unsuitable clothing with no provision for emergencies and take it for granted that the Mountain Rescue Team will come to their aid if they find themselves in trouble.

Apparently some people do this time and time again . . .

Call Out the Mountain Rescue!

Call out the Mountain Rescue!
I came up for a lark,
But the night is getting chilly,
And the fells are getting dark,
My shoe's lost its stiletto heel,
My frock is feeling thin,
Call out the Mountain Rescue,
And let's get taken in.

Call out the Mountain Rescue!
To search the hills and vales,
Swathed in ropes and cables,
Like a team of Chippendales,*
Release the search-and-rescue dogs!
They'll find me by my smell,
I ate a Kendal Mint Cake,
And I'm wearing my Chanel.

Call out the Mountain Rescue!
I am stranded on a crag,
My hairstyle's badly damaged
And I snapped my shoulder-bag,
I'm utterly exhausted,
Cannot move another inch,
So hail the helicopter!
I am ready for the winch.

Call out the Mountain Rescue,
Wrap me warm and well,
Lay me on a stretcher bed,
And bear me down the fell,
Heal me with your tenderness,
Drench me with your sorrow,
Drop me off at home,
I'll call you out again tomorrow.

*A raunchy American male stripper act.

Walking to Falkirk

During the last century Highland cattle, having reached maturity on the island of Skye, would be taken to the cattle markets of Falkirk on the mainland. The only way for them to get there was to walk and when they reached the intervening stretch of water, they were made to swim. A rope passing beneath the tongue was secured around the lower jaw and the animals were towed behind rowing boats to reach the mainland.

I like Highland cattle with their thick fringes, wide horns and ponderous faces, and I think they would have found this treatment a serious affront to their dignity . . .

Walking to Falkirk

I am just not looking forward to this journey to Falkirk,
I have tried to get excited but I can't, it doesn't work,
Three hundred miles of walking south, *walking* night and day!
Plodding over Scotland, udders swinging all the way.

Well I'm not going, I'm not going, as a rule I'm kind and nice,
But I'm not built for endurance, I won't go at any price.

Well, what a thing to ask of me, of me and all my friends,
Imagine our discomfort as we hobble through the glens,
The flies! The deprivations! And as if that weren't enough,
We'd have to eat the heather, and it's stringy! And it's tough!

So I'm not going! I'm not going, I won't plunge or go berserk,
But I'm no long-distance runner, I'm not walking to Falkirk.

Now it's come to my attention that upon the drovers' whim,
They tip us in the briny and encourage us to *swim*!
I'd have no shred of dignity! I'm much too highly strung
To be *towed* behind a rowboat with a rope beneath my
     tongue!

No, I'm not going, I'm not walking, I'm not flailing through
     the mud,
I'll be found beneath my shady tree, chewing on the cud.

In fact I've ruminated here from underneath my fringe,
And have devised a policy to make the drover cringe,
So when he comes for me, one of these frosty Highland
     morns,
I'll be waiting with a welcome! With a welcome from my
     horns!

Yes, see the drover fly! There go his sporran and his dirk,
'Cause I'm not walking, I'm not walking, I'm NOT
     WALKING to Falkirk.

Glasses

I have to wear glasses now, for reading. I did think I wasn't going to be like everybody else, but I am of course. While I'm very grateful to the opticians' art for giving me a means to go on reading at all, I find I feel no affection for my glasses because I can never *find* the damn things. I traipse round the house looking for them. Did I leave them in the kitchen? No. Perhaps I left them upstairs by the bed. Not there? Well, what about by my armchair when I was watching TV? No? Round and round I go.

I feel enraged at the ludicrous amount of time I'm wasting looking for my glasses, but at the same time a rising panic because I can't manage without the things. When I eventually find them I feel in such a state, I could twist and mangle them to nothing.

My family don't help. They never say, 'How frustrating for you, Mother, where might you have had them last?' Oh no, none of that. They all shout, 'Oh God, not *again*, you haven't lost them *again*! Why don't you hang them round your neck?'

Well, I could. If I wanted to. I've got one of those fancy chains whereby you can indeed hang them round your neck. Only I feel matronly in them. I don't like it. When you bend over they swing out in front of you. The glasses. With a pair of varifocals hanging round my neck I don't feel like the cool poetry chick that I know I truly am.

If I Only Had My Glasses,
I'd Be There

I was decorating recently, the paper it was hung,
I was balanced on the ladder, on the very topmost rung,
I was snipping round the switches, I was sticking up the frieze,
But then I overreached myself and fell and hurt my knees.

But if I'd only had my glasses I'd be there,
Doing snowy ceilings high above the stair,
I wouldn't lie here in the drips,
Looking upward at the rips,
If I'd only had my glasses, I'd be there.

I had a few days' holiday and went to catch the train,
I tried to read the timetable, it wasn't very plain,
The numbers they were minuscule, the writing was so small,
My final destination wasn't where I hoped at all.

But if I'd only had my glasses, I'd be there,
At the seaside with the ozone in my hair,
I wouldn't walk this night so dank,
Trying to find a taxi rank,
If I'd only had my glasses, I'd be there.

This morning I went riding on my bike, it was a treat,
The pedals they were flying as I hurtled down the street,
Men were doing excavations and I never saw the pit,
Now my bike and I are parted and I'm lying in the grit.

But if I'd only had my glasses I'd be there,
I'd be bicycling away without a care,
I'd not be lying here supine,
Because I didn't see the sign,
If I'd only had my glasses I'd be there.

An old flame came to visit me, I trembled, it was *him*!
The years had not been brutal, he was handsome still, and slim,
The flames of love still flickered as he stretched his arms out wide,
And with a breathless utterance, I ran straight round the side.

But if I'd only had my glasses I'd be there,
If I'd remembered where I'd put a pair
I could be gazing at him now,
Well, squinting at him anyhow,
If I'd only had my glasses, I'd be there!

Adopting a Dog

Our dog died. We had her for twelve years. She came from a dogs' home startlingly named The Sombrero, in Droitwich, where she was optimistically described as a 'Labrador type'. When our two small sons were growing up, there was always a threesome, two little boys and a dog, with a ball or stick for the entertainment of all parties. Years later she became ill and frail and one morning we came downstairs and found she had died.

I always keep a towel for each of my dogs, to dry them when they come in wet, so we wrapped her up in her own blue towel. My sons dug a grave for her in the orchard and we buried her and everybody cried. What touched me so much was the tenderness with which my great eighteen-year-old son arranged the towel across her face so that the soil wouldn't go into her eyes. By a dismal piece of timing, that night I had five hundred people in a theatre in Essex waiting for a good laugh.

After a time we got used to the idea that she had gone but we all missed our big dog, and our Jack Russell terrier Tatty was lonely and had nobody to stand underneath. She's called Tatty because every hair that grows in her coat comes out at a different angle. My husband says she looks like a lavatory brush. We had space for another large dog and knew that the dogs' homes are full of brilliant pets waiting for another chance, so I drove up to the Blue Cross at nearby Burford to see what dogs were available.

It's a fairly new place. Viewed from above, it looks like a cake with the actual kennels in the centre and the runs radiating out like wedges, so you can walk all the way round and see the dogs inside. Some runs have two dogs, others only one, and there are balls and rubber bones lying around but they don't seem to get played with much.

Some dogs looked savage and snarled, others seemed cowed and frightened. I came to a great smiling golden retriever called Hattie who waved her fine tail, but when I asked about her I found she had just been adopted by another family. I went back out and walked round until I came to a different dog. I stopped. It barked nervously at me. It was a very odd-looking dog. Immensely tall and spindly, with long black ears, a black saddle and strange dappled spots, it was painfully thin with the bumps of its spine sticking up all along its back. Round the run was a blue-and-white cordon like the ones the police put round a crime scene, and on it someone had written in black felt-tip pen: 'Do not approach this dog. This dog may have ringworm.' Other people passing exclaimed with distaste and nervousness, '*Ringworm*.' The dog stood in a shallow puddle of disinfectant in the newly cleansed run, and looked the most lonely, heart-broken, baffled animal I had ever seen. I thought: 'That dog looks daft enough to be our dog!'

I went back into the office and enquired about it. I said: 'I like the look of that black-and-white mongrel, the one that might have ringworm.'

The man said, 'Oh no, dear, oh no. That dog is no mongrel. *She* is a LARGE MUNSTERLANDER.'

I looked at him blankly. I had never heard of it. Apparently it is a German gun-dog breed, developed in and around the area of Munster.

I said, 'What's her name?'

The man said, 'Ella.'

I thought about it. 'I don't like that name much, for a dog. It's sort of wishy-washy. If I had her, do you think I could call her something else?'

'Oh yes, dear,' he said, 'you can call her anything you like but she won't know who you're talking to.'

That made perfectly good sense. I told him that we would like to offer her a home.

Now, if you adopt a dog from a dogs' home, you are not allowed to just clip on a lead and walk out with it. Many of the dogs have had a poor start for one reason or another, so the staff need to feel fairly sure that you will be a better bet, that you and the dog will suit each other. To this end you are asked to comply with several procedures. First they like to see any other dogs which live in your home, and introduce them to the new dog on neutral ground to see if they are going to get along, or detest each other. Somewhat nervously I went home and fetched Tatty. She marched in, chest out, saying, 'The bigger they come, the harder they fall . . .' but on seeing the stupendous size of the other dog, she decided to be friendly. They ran after a ball together and didn't fall out.

Next, you are asked to bring in all the members of the family who live at home. You stand in a line and they look in your ears to see if you've got canker. No, I made that up, they don't do that really; they just like to meet everyone, I suppose to see if there are any dissenters. After that an inspector comes out to your home to see if your garden is secure, that the dog can't get out on to a busy road for instance, and they check other possible hazards. Eventually all this was done and we were told that we could have Ella. We had to wait for her to be spayed as it's the policy of the home to neuter all dogs, and one day we went in our car to collect her and bring her home duly embroidered.

When we got her home I began to realise just what we had taken on. She was ten months old and had received no training at all. She took no notice of anything you said to her, she wasn't clean and she stole food. If you were unwise enough to leave a delicious roast leg of lamb on the worktop she would stroll up and, enabled by her enormous height, help herself and say, 'Well, this is dashed good of the old gal.'

One day I made a Victoria sandwich. I had a lot of people coming to tea so I doubled the recipe to make a big one. On the beautiful fluted golden-brown base I spread thickly whipped double cream. Over that I smoothed a generous layer of my own blackcurrant jam. One ran down over the other in a voluptuous dribble. Then I positioned the lovely golden top, placed the cake on a pretty china stand and dredged the whole glorious edifice with a snowy dusting of icing sugar. It was a work of art. It looked like a picture in a magazine. I left it on the worktop and went upstairs to get the washing.

When I came down I honestly thought I was seeing things. It was a scene of utter desecration. The whole cake had been smashed down on to the floor and reduced to a swirled creamy mess of chunks, crumbs and jammy paw prints. The big dog, her long black nose covered in cream back to the eyes, was saying, 'It was nothing to do with me. I don't eat cake.' Tatty, moustache bristling with crumbs, was saying, 'Quick! Get some more down here!'

I decided I needed some help. I rang the vet, explained the situation and asked if he knew of a good dog trainer.

'This lady seems to be well thought of,' he said. 'I'll give you the number.'

I rang the lady and told her about Ella. She paused, fetched her diary and said, yes, she could come out on Thursday and train me. Me, you notice.

On Thursday she duly arrived and I was taken aback. She came in a big truck and was herself a large, forthright woman.

'Morning!' she boomed. 'Morning, Mrs Russell!'

Russell is my married name. My husband has been called Mr Ayres for twenty-three years and it gets on his wick.

She inspected the dog and announced: 'Now, the first thing I observe about your dog, Mrs Russell, is that your dog does not come back when you call it!'

I had observed that for myself.

'As such,' she went on, 'your dog is a menace to itself and to everybody else! So today we will work on the Recall. THE RECALL! I want you to attach your dog to a long rope and then I want you to SPRINT across the field in the direction of the OAK TREE, while BLOWING your WHISTLE, and calling your dog's name ENTHUSIASTICALLY! When you reach the

tree I want you to BOB DOWN and PROFFER THE TITBIT!
OFF YOU GO!'

Well, I didn't know if I was on foot or horseback. The dog
was so immensely strong she nearly pulled my arm OFF. I was
trying to blow the whistle and gasp out the dog's name at the
same time, while behind me the lady shrilled, 'She can't HEAR
you!' I rushed across the field, ducked down behind the tree and
ate the titbit by mistake. It was a nightmare. I felt so unco-
ordinated and humiliated. This went on for three weeks. At the
end of the three weeks it was decided that I would now continue
on my own and try to put into practice what I had been shown.
That was the situation when a terrible thing happened.

My husband had gone out with the dog last thing at night for
a wee. For the dog. I thought they had been gone a long time
and I began to have misgivings. After far too long a time the
back door was kicked open. In came my husband all red in the
face. He was blazing. His eyes stood out. He exploded: 'The
bloody dog's run off!'

Then, well you can guess what came next, he shouted:
'I never wanted the BLOODY DOG in THE FIRST PLACE!'

'Oh no? Well, you might have mentioned that before NOW!'

Anyway the dog had gone. She's a gun dog who had spent the
first ten months of her life in London starved of any of the
exciting scents she was bred to respond to. All round us there
are multitudes of rabbits and foxes. She had just put her head
down, broken the collar and vanished.

The whole family rushed outside. It was late at night and
foggy. Everywhere was a still silence. There was no yelp, no
excited bark, no helpful snapping of twigs under excited paws.
There was nothing, only fog and deadly quiet. It was terrible.

We came in. I phoned the police and the dog warden in
Swindon. We live surrounded by livestock. For all I knew, our

dog could have been dragging the throats out of all the neigh-
bouring sheep. Or our own sheep. It was terrifying. The whole
family at that late hour went out to look for her. My husband
went off in his car and our two sons went off in their various
vehicles. I could see their headlights in the fog, criss-crossing the
surrounding fields, driving slowly along the edges of woods. We
searched all night. I was the last to give up at a quarter to five in
the morning. Prior to that I had been walking along the local
roads with a big torch, shouting: 'ACHTUNG! Where are you,
you great BRATWURST, come home!'

We never found her ourselves. She came home by herself
filthy and exhausted at about eleven o'clock the next morning.
She must have run for miles and miles.

That was the low point. Since then things have steadily
improved and now you wouldn't recognise her. She has turned
into one of those admirable, eager-to-please dogs which do as
they are told, and the touching thing is that she *loves* my hus-
band. She absolutely adores him. She didn't hear what he said
about her that night.

When he comes in from work at night he is tired. He doesn't
want to dance the salsa, he's weary. He likes to have his supper
and sit down with the paper. He's got a green leather reclining
armchair and he likes to sit with his feet up, cup of coffee on
one side, paper on the other, TV in front, and he's perfectly
happy. The dog watches him carefully until he is settled. Then,
sinuous and snake-like, she pussyfoots over to him and lies
down in a great curving arc close beside him. She rolls over on
to her back with her four great hooves in the air and gazes up at
him with an expression of utter devotion.

Unfortunately she is a martyr to flatulence, and this can
rather spoil the effect. Sometimes my husband doesn't have to
turn the pages of the newspaper himself at all. Nevertheless,

despite all this, I still have two dogs and one husband under the same roof.

I hope my account has not discouraged you from adopting your own dog from a dogs' home. Ours has been well worth the effort.

Bonemeal

Bury me beside my dogs,
The dogs I loved and knew,
So, as in life, they'll never be
Short of a bone to chew.

A Place in the Sun

I like the idea of sunbathing in the garden but somehow the reality never quite lives up to the mental picture. I think, 'Well, it looks glorious out there, I'll put the old sun lounger out on the lawn and read the paper for a while. After all, you wait all year for this weather, don't you? All those months shut up, all those dreary winter days. Yes! Let's go for it!'

So I drag the sun lounger out of the back of the garage on to the lawn and beat off the worst of the dust. It's an old-fashioned fat padded job where you have to draw out a concealed extension to support your legs. Once you get on, it's a struggle to get back up. Anyway, I erect the thing, lie on it and start reading the paper.

Well, it's bright. I mean my eyes aren't what they used to be anyway, and the bright sun on the paper is too much for me. This doesn't matter, however, because I do have a pair of prescription sunglasses. Somewhere.

I get off the lounger, put my shoes back on, go indoors and search all through my little drawers and cupboards to find the glasses. Eventually, I do find them and go back out to the lawn. In my absence a mischievous breeze has sprung up and blown my newspaper all round the garden. Sheets are pasted against the garden wall and various shrubs. I retrieve them all, stepping over the plants like a hackney trotter. Now I've got my paper and my prescription sunglasses and I sit back down to relax at last.

But it's hot. Really hot. I can feel it on my collar-bone and on those knobbly bits at the front where you know the skin is perilously thin. I know I'm going to wake up in the morning with my skin that obscene blue colour which means that you've really burned yourself. I lived in Singapore for a couple of years and there they used to say that bad sunburn hurts most for the first four days. Well, I don't want to have to put up with *that*.

I know there's a bottle of sunscreen lotion in the house. Somewhere. Ratty now, I rise up out of the lounger and go to fetch it. It's upstairs in the bathroom at the back of the cluttered cabinet. I find it and take it outside, plaster it over my front and shoulders, hating the greasiness and brothel-like perfume. I lie back, put the glasses on, take up the paper and stretch out in the sun.

I leap with fear, as if electrified, as the dog suddenly starts to bark. She's up, her hackles are up, she disappears towards the front of the house barking in one continuous wailing howl. It's a well-known fact that most burglaries take place at around three o'clock in the afternoon. I look at my watch. It's three o'clock in the afternoon. I go and have a look. It's nothing, a cat or some pleasant person bringing the parish newsletter. Back on the sun lounger I know the moment has passed when through the open kitchen window I hear the phone start to ring. Enough's enough. With my greasy fingers I gather up the sunscreen, glasses, cardigan, pair of shoes, cup of tea and newspaper, kick the sun lounger over and go indoors.

The Battle of Portaloo

We had the builders in and they brought a Portaloo. I found it rather an affront, standing in my garden. It was a violent blue and not what I wanted to look at. Whenever I went outside to be spiritually uplifted by my flowers there it was, usually with the door hanging open, the inside moulded in grim grey plastic. Several times when the breeze was up, interleaved toilet paper blew all over the yard. I grew to dislike it. When it was occupied, smoke came out of the louvres round the roof and a tinny radio could be heard from within. I was glad when it was loaded on to the back of a pick-up truck and borne, still at a drunken angle, down our drive, out on to the main road and away.

The Battle of Portaloo

Shut that Portaloo door up, boys, shut that Portaloo do,
Well, I like the look of a great many things but I ain't so sure
    about you.
No. I want to see my garden, boys, the beautiful flowers I've
    grown,
So shut that Portaloo door up, boys, I don't want to see that
    throne.

No. I don't like that Portaloo, boys, it's not my favourite
    sight,
It's leaning over sideways painted horrible blue and white,
It's gaudy and it's bawdy and the sight of it makes me
    cringe,
Standing in the rubble with the door coming off of its
    hinge.

So, close that chemical cavern up, boys, you hide that tissue
    paper roll,
Well, I don't want to be looking at those things when I go for
    a stroll,
And don't puff any more fags in there, boys, don't puff those
    cigars,
She's smoking like a rocket ship, on her way to Mars.

Now the carpenter's gone and the search is on and the
   swearing makes me wince,
Well, he disappeared an hour ago and they have not seen him
   since.
They're searching and they're cursing but he didn't go that far,
He's hid from view in the Portaloo with a fag and the *Daily
   Star*.

Now I'm not averse to toilets, boys, I use one every day,
But I don't want to goggle at yours, I s'pose I'm funny that
   way.
I'm tired of the click-click polythene roof expanding in the
   sun,
And tired of the radio, clack-clack chit-chat, tuned to Radio 1.

So. Load that Portaloo up now, boys, you lever it up on the
   van,
Well, I used to be a tolerant gal, but that's all gone down the
   pan.
I like a tasteful toilet, boys, I like a loo that knows its place,
But I don't like that Portaloo, boys, it's all too 'in your face'.

So a fond adieu to the Portaloo, and I hope that you're gone
   for good,
There's only a whiff of disinfectant showing us where you
   stood,
And so, my friends, these cigarette ends they mark the noble
   site,
Where the underpaid of the building trade went . . . for a brief
   respite.

The Nasty Cornish Pastie

The photo on the recipe, I saw it and rejoiced,
The pastry it was golden and the filling it was moist,
I gathered the ingredients, I couldn't wait to try,
But I reckon down in Cornwall, they must like their pasties
    dry,
It was drier than the desert, it was drier than the dust,
It was one cube of potato in a monumental crust,
The filling must have vaporised, it made you catch your
    breath,
I had baked a Cornish pastie that could choke a man to death.

Shopping on the Internet

Our two sons are both six feet five inches tall, and don't they eat! Extraordinary amounts of food come into our house and disappear in a flash. At home I've got one of those big fridges with double doors. At regular intervals a great son will march in, wrench open the doors, rest his arms along the top and rock backwards and forwards like a giant vulture whilst peering into the depths of the fridge with an expression of acute disappointment because there's never anything in there. This is because I go out and do a big shop, they come home and do a big eat, and then it's all over.

One day I gave myself a talking-to. Why, I wondered, was it that I was still prepared to run around the supermarket doing all this shopping, struggling home and up the path laden and exhausted? Surely nowadays any busy, thinking woman ordered it all on the internet, and watched somebody else wrestle it into the house? I asked myself if I was prepared to be left behind, to ignore the new technology, to become an old fogey in a time warp. No, I said, I wasn't.

Admittedly I was nervous but I set about ordering a weekly shop on the unfamiliar internet. I decided to buy the basics: coffee, bread, tea, milk, all the stuff we ran out of. The only unusual item was a weekly tub of a particular salad which my sons liked, a mixture of mozzarella, sun-dried tomatoes, pine nuts and pesto. I included it as a small treat from their fond mother.

When I'd finished ordering my groceries, I went back to the beginning and scrolled down (as we computer-literate people say) just to check that everything looked all right. I was aghast to see one item priced at £7,000. I had a closer look and could see what had happened. Not only am I not knowledgeable about computers, I'm not very clued up on metrication either. It was the fancy salad. I thought I'd ordered 400 grams, whereas in fact I had actually asked for 400 *kilos*! Had I not spotted the mistake, I could have taken delivery of a whole lorry-load.

Don't let my small oversight put you off, though. I can now order a weekly internet shop with cool confidence. Irritatingly, no sooner had I cracked it, than our two sons found jobs and left home. Now my husband and I can carry our small weekly requirements home in a carrier bag.

There's Some Mistake

Mirror, mirror, on the wall,
Where am I? I'm young and tall,
I'm not like that old bird at all,
There's some mistake . . .
So that old gal, I say again,
Is much too old and much too plain,
With glasses on a chain!
For goodness sake . . .

Mirror, mirror softly lit,
Where is my husband strong and fit?
Raconteur and wit,
There's some mistake . . .

I know my man and he's not it,
That bald and boring stooped old git,
He looks about to quit,
Give him a shake.

Where are my children young and free,
So beautiful for all to see?
They are not here with me,
There's some mistake . . .
They're scattered now, gone to achieve,
With partners I could take or leave,
In silent rooms I grieve
For old times' sake.

The old grim reaper's on his way,
To cut his corn; to make his hay,
The closing of the day,
And no mistake.
He runs his thumb along the blade,
And steps towards me from the shade,
I think I've overstayed
And start to quake . . .

Mirror, mirror, on the wall,
I don't like what I see at all,
You're heading for a fall,
You need a break.
So stand well back and mind the crash,
Here's the brick and there's the smash,
See? Younger in a flash,
A piece of cake.

Job Applicant

SCENE
Interior shabby Soho office. Distant traffic. Flies buzzing.

CHARACTERS
GEOFF: a seedy agent
PAM: a plain middle-aged woman

Knock on door:

GEOFF: Come in.

PAM: Morning. Is this the Starlight job agency?

GEOFF: Yes.

PAM: I've got your advert here in *The Stage*. It says 'Always seeking good-looking girls, glamorous work on cruise ships and in exotic destinations.'

GEOFF: Right.

PAM: Well, I'd like to apply for the job.

GEOFF: What job? Cleaning? Catering?

PAM: Oh no, no, nothing like that.

GEOFF: Well, what?

PAM: Pole dancer.

GEOFF: Pole dancer?

PAM: Yes. I had the hip replacement in April, so as long as I held on to the pole with both hands, I could manage the pelvic thrust.

GEOFF: Is this a wind-up?

PAM: It most certainly is not. My husband thinks it's a marvellous idea. He's a Pole.

GEOFF: I can't believe I'm having this conversation. You're about forty years too old!

PAM: Yes, well I thought you might think that. But I've been watching the blokes who go into these pole-dancing clubs. And they're old. There's not a young feller amongst them. They're all old crocks.

GEOFF: Well what makes you think they'd want to look at you?

PAM: Well, I'm homely. Those young girls are laughing at them really. They smile at them but their hearts are full of contempt. Now with me, they'd see things that would make them feel at home.

GEOFF: Like what?

PAM: Well, thread veins, sagging flesh, dropsy.

GEOFF: Yeah, well, I don't think so.

PAM: And when I shake a leg they'd hear something they recognise!

GEOFF: Don't tell me. What?

PAM: The joint crack!

GEOFF: I don't have to listen to this drivel. I've got good-looking gullible girls coming in here all the time begging me to find them work.

PAM: Well, you tell them there's a vacancy at Lil's lap-dancing club in Wallingford Street.

GEOFF: Yeah? And how would you know that?

PAM: I had to hand in my notice. None of the punters had a lap big enough.

Mixed Ward

The gentleman across from me,
Is quite a jolly sort.
His nightshirt's rather skimpy,
And his legs are rather short.
He flings one to the left-hand side,
The other to the right,
Last time I saw a sight like that,
Was on my wedding night.

The Packing Poem

I was invited to go to a smart hotel and resort in Malindi, Kenya. It's a place where people go to relax on intensely white beaches or to take up a mighty rod and go game fishing. Over Christmas and the New Year the hotel takes in its full capacity of guests, then closes the doors and offers them all manner of luxurious food and amenities.

Various speakers and entertainers are shipped in and I was invited to go and perform my show on a beautiful African evening under the stars. All my family were invited for the eight-day trip and we were filled with happy anticipation.

I had just one problem: I didn't know what to pack. I knew it was going to be outlandishly hot so that whatever I took needed to be cool, and I also knew that it was a malarial area so that garments worn in the evening should cover the arms. Additionally, the hotel guests would be well-heeled and in their Christmas finery, so I wanted to look appropriately dressed, but not as if I was trying to outshine the audience.

Well, I was in a panic. I didn't seem to have anything that would fit the bill. Nothing cool had sleeves. I fell into the trap where, not knowing whether to take this one or that one, you take them both. Keep doing that and you end up as I did, with an enormous selection of clothes that might do. These I stuffed into a vast green suitcase, which my two poor sons staggered around with in the tropical steaming heat of Africa, grunting, 'You, Mother, are a right pillock!'

They were right, I was. When the proprietor of the hotel came out to greet us, he looked at my suitcase and said, 'Oh. I see you travel light.' I was a laughing-stock and deservedly so. Predictably, when the entire tonnage of clothing returned home, I had worn just a tiny fraction of it. I felt foolish because I'd got it so wrong. I've done a lot of travelling and should have been more efficient.

However, talking to my girlfriends later, I was comforted to find that their attitude was fairly flippant. 'Oh yeah,' each one nodded, 'I always do that, take a load of stuff and never wear it, bring it all back home again. Everybody does, don't worry about it.'

I'm always on the lookout for new things to write about so I thought I would tackle this subject of packing.

The Packing Poem

I'm packing for my holiday, I want to take enough
Of cotton underclothing, swimming wear, sarongs and stuff.
I take my own shampoo, conditioner and my own hair-drier,
I don't trust those hotel ones not to set your hair on fire.
I take insect repellent, both the lotion and the spray,
They make you smell of creosote but keep the bugs away.
You only get one skin and I shall take good care of mine,
By packing all this sun protection, factor ninety-nine.

Right. That's filled up one suitcase and I'm only taking two.
For holidaying *anywhere* you need a comfy shoe,
So it's sandals for the sunny weather, walkers when it's cool,
Flatties for sightseeing and some flip-flops for the pool,
Higher heels for evening but these make my ankles ache,
So I'll take some lower strappy ones in case they're a mistake.
My feet look neglected, well I look at them and sigh,
But it's been so cold I haven't really seen them since July.

Women with attractive feet will look at mine and scoff,
So I'll take some nail polish and some stuff to take it off,
Clippers, moisturiser and a piece of pumice stone,
So I can rasp the soles when I am safely on my own.
Oh, that's filled up this suitcase so I'll have to take the three,
But taking one half-full seems very sensible to me,
When you've hit the local markets, you've got spaces free and
     clear,
To pop in every keepsake, knick-knack, gift and souvenir.

Now, moving on to clothing, I shall keep it cool and light,
With something warm in case it turns out chilly on the flight,
I'll need a coat for going to the airport, there and back,
Then again it could be raining so I'll have to take a mack,
But let's not think of rain! Let's think of sunshine hot and
     strong!
My poor old pasty body's been wrapped up for far too long.
In goes my wide-brimmed hat which set me back by fifty quid,
And my wraparound sunglasses so I look like Jodie Kidd.

Now, cotton dresses, sleeved and sleeveless, spotted, plain and
     checked,
I'll pack a few of each and then at least I'll be correct.

Trousers, light and dark with an elasticated band,
So I can eat too much, sit back and let it all expand,
I'm taking lots of shorts, they're just the thing for everyday,
Though these look better from the front than when I walk
    away,
So I'd better take the medium, the skimpy and the long,
So whatever length I need, I'll have them all and won't go
    wrong.

Now my other small conundrum is, how dressy will it be?
I don't want a situation where the odd one out is *me*,
But if I pack something glamorous and pull out every stop,
I could look like a Christmas tree and well over the top.
I'll have to strike a compromise, take something in-between,
This dress is black, unfussy, very classical and clean,
I'll take a filmy wrap to make it look a bit more swell,
And this wrap's nice, and that one, and I'll take those two as
    well!

Oh. That's filled up that suitcase so I'll have to take the four,
It's getting rather difficult to move across the floor,
But they're necessary items, all essential for the trip,
I tell less-travelled friends: 'Don't over-pack! You take my tip.'
Finally, the traveller's cheques, the tickets, cards and cash,
Earplugs, if the passenger next door talks balderdash,
My little bits of jewellery all done up in a roll,
Ten blockbuster novels and my paracetamol.

Just a few more incidentals, glasses, cameras and clocks,
Passport, medication and a pair of special socks
To prevent deep vein thrombosis, I've been wearing them all
    day,

What amazing blissful comfort, they're just like a tourniquet.
That's it. I'm packed and ready. What a woman, what a star!
My husband's coming up to take the cases to the car,
He's bounding up the stairs, he's here, he's opening the door,
Taken one look at the luggage and collapsed upon the floor!

Chorleywood

I disappoint people because they expect me to be able to write apt things at the drop of a hat, and I can't. I think that to be funny about someone, you have to know the small details about them, all their little idiosyncrasies. The idea of writing something hilarious about a person you've never met is nonsense to me. I wouldn't know where to start.

'Dash off' is the term used. It crops up a lot in radio stations: 'Here, Pam, dash off something quick about our presenter. That'll give him a surprise!'

I did try to do it for a while, early on. One of the first professional engagements I had was an interview with the radio DJ Steve Wright on the beach at Weston-super-Mare. He was presenting a pop music roadshow and was broadcasting from a special trailer on the sands. Crowds of young people were sitting around in the sunshine enjoying being part of the broadcast.

Inside the trailer I was nervously waiting to be interviewed by Steve Wright when the producer of the programme suddenly said to me, 'There are about two minutes before the end of this track, Pam, could you just *dash off* a little verse about Steve? Doesn't have to be much, just a couple of lines? You've got about a minute and a half . . .'

Nowadays I'd just say 'Sorry, 'fraid not,' but then I was anxious to co-operate at any cost so I came up with:

> *Steve plays all kinds of music,*
> *Rock, soul and honky-tonky,*
> *And if you don't like any of that,*
> *You can go for a ride on a donkey!*

Just think what I could have written if I'd had *five* minutes!

Recently I was working in New Zealand. My husband and I were flying down to Christchurch in the South Island and I noticed that the lady flight attendant at the front of the plane seemed to be scrutinising me. She came over.

'Excuse me,' she said, 'I know you've seen me looking at you and I don't want to embarrass you, but I must ask, are you Pam Ayres?'

I said, 'Yes, I am, that's right.'

'Oh, I thought you were!' she confided. 'I thought it was you!'

I smiled and nodded and then she said:

'Tell me, do you still write limericks? Isn't that what you *used to do*?'

I said, 'Yes, that's right, that's what I used to do,' but in my heart I thought, 'Yes, and I'm still at it, Sunshine, and better than ever!'

She went back to her den at the front. After a time she returned looking excited. 'I've just been talking to the Captain!' she enthused. 'He wondered if you'd like to write a little funny verse about him. He comes from Chorleywood!'

Despite this nugget of crucial information it was hopeless, and I did my usual explanation about not being able to write about somebody if I didn't know them. The atmosphere became somewhat scornful and frosty.

'Oh I see. Well, that *is* surprising. Never mind then. I thought you'd be able to manage *that*.'

It was quite a long flight down to Christchurch and I found

myself turning the conundrum over in my mind. In the end I did come up with a little verse but I thought I would be better keeping it to myself:

> *I am the jolly pilot,*
> *I come from Chorleywood,*
> *Could you land the aeroplane?*
> *'Cause I'm not very good.*

The Akaroa Cannon

See the town of Akaroa in a great volcanic bay,
Where from Christchurch in New Zealand people drive out
    for the day,
To eat in wooden cafés with their stripped and sanded floor,
And close beside the jetty there's a cannon on the shore.

A cannon set by city fathers some forgotten day,
Squats upon the grass and faces out across the bay,
An interesting artefact, a piece of history,
But the Akaroa cannon is significant to me.

For I came here many years ago, I had two little sons,
And they were most attracted to all weaponry and guns,
They fell upon the cannon with excitement and delight,
And imaginary cannonballs went flying in the night.

Then I was their needed mother in the role I loved the best,
And the fullness of fulfilment rose and sparkled in my chest,
I put my arms around them in their innocence and youth,
And to keep them safe from harm I would have died, and
    that's the truth.

Now I'm back in Akaroa and my little birds have flown,
They're swimming in the cut and thrust, surviving on their
    own,
At work in weary cities with a mortgage and a boss,
And I'm standing by the cannon and my heart is pierced with
    loss.

Now the breeze across the ocean is more cutting; cold and
    chill,
Just a band of muffled tourists straggle on the boardwalk still,
But my sons are on the barrel, lit up, laughing all the day,
Of the Akaroa cannon,
As I turn and walk away.

At the Hairdresser

Do you know what I miss when I'm away from home? My hairdresser. I know it sounds a bit feeble and girlie but I do. I don't want that much, I just want to feel that I look like me, and my normal hairdresser gets on and does it.

Going to a different hairdresser can be quite intimidating. I once fled in fear from a salon in Edinburgh where all the employees wore black leather and had facial piercings.

New hairdressers can feel that they should engage you in conversation, so you get the interrogation that goes: 'Do you live round here? Going out tonight? Had your holidays?' etc. Maybe I'm crabby but I like to sit quietly and read a magazine. That is a treat for me.

I was working in Australia a while ago and my hair was a sight. I'd had various unwise things done to it. It was dry like straw, a mean yellow colour, and too short. I couldn't make it look right, couldn't make it look like *me*. I was worried because I was touring Australia and appearing on TV to promote the tour, trying to persuade people that they should come to see me. For that you want to feel you look your best and I certainly didn't.

I mentioned this to the woman I was working with. I said, 'I don't know *what* I'm going to do with my hair. It's a real mess and I don't know where to go to get it sorted out.'

She said, 'Don't worry. I'll make you an appointment with my hairdresser. He's marvellous. He'll fit you in, as it's you. He's not a hairdresser. He's a *sculptor*. Wait till you walk into his place. It's like Spot the Celeb!'

I wasn't sure this sounded like my sort of place but I had no other ideas, so accepted gratefully and went along at the appointed time. Once inside I was approached by the sculptor, who turned out to be a small man of Mediterranean appearance and who, for reasons I did not understand, had intertwined into his own hair, a tea towel. He was very slim. If my father had seen him he would have said, ''E looks like a matchstick with the wood shaved off.' Anyway I was whisked off and shampooed in a decadent horizontal position, lying on a couch.

On being delivered back to the sculptor, he sprayed a great crackling ball of mousse into his hands and clawed it through my hair. I don't like that stuff much, it makes my hair sticky, but on it went. He then blow-dried it, and towards the end of the process asked me to put my head between my knees as if I had fainted, which I was shortly about to do. He then ran his fingers through my hair from the nape to the crown, in little fishy movements, while assuming a strange other-worldly expression. Nothing was said. It was bizarre. At last he stood back with outstretched arms as if to say, '*Voilà!*'

I straightened up with the utmost trepidation and studied my reflection in the mirror. It was ludicrous. I looked as if I had been out in a hurricane. My hair was stiff and hard and stuck out at wild angles. I looked for all the world like a woman with her finger in the socket.

I knew straight away what I should have said.

I should have said, 'See here, Ferdinand! I don't know what you think you're playing at but this looks absurd. It's awful! It's hard and stiff and all stuck out at different angles. It's not what I asked for, it doesn't suit me, and I want it put right NOW, AT YOUR EXPENSE!'

That's what I should have said.

In actual fact I said: 'Oh, it's very nice, thank you very much.' And to crown it all, I went off and left him a tip.

Hair, Proper Hair

You may love it, you may hate it,
You may oil and lubricate it,
You may cosset it with every type of cure,
You may curl it, you may crimp it,
Stick a toupee like a limpet
On the top of it but still you may be sure . . .

We need hair to cut a dash,
Hair to shimmer, gleam and flash,
Hair to tenderly administer and groom,
Hair to curl, hair to plait,
Hair to complement your hat
For turning heads when walking in a room . . .

You need hair, proper hair,
It's the only thing to wear,
And for Royalty it's simply de rigueur,
As a crown from noble kin
Won't look half as good on skin
And the Queen responded when we asked of her . . .

(*Queenly voice*): One needs hair, proper hair,
To hold tiaras square,
One's hair is understated and discreet,
In one's subjects one expects
To see hair about their necks
As they sing 'God Save the Queen' and line the streets.

MBE

At last they've recognised my charms
I've ordered up the coat of arms
Bought myself an ermine cape
Told the kids to bow and scrape
Carved on the door for all to see:
The legend, Pam Ayres, MBE.

Heart to Heart

Pam and her friend Felicity. Two middle-aged friends chatting in the kitchen over a coffee:

PAM: You know, Felicity, what I hated about the old days when I was growing up was how repressed people were. Human relationships were never discussed, not like today. It was ridiculous. What are the main things about life, eh? I'll tell you. Birth, death and . . . you know . . . birth, death and um . . . er . . .

FELICITY: Sex

PAM: Exactly. But when I was growing up it was NEVER talked about. It didn't matter how awful the problem was, if it . . . you know, if it was anything to do with . . . um . . .

FELICITY: Sexual relations.

PAM: It was a no-no. Not mentioned. They ran a mile. Even when I got married, my mother never told me anything. She just said, 'Now, you're going to have to confront your husband's . . . um . . . your husband's . . . um . . .'

FELICITY: Requirements.

PAM: Requirements, that's right. But there was no advice. She was so embarrassed. She said, 'You may find your husband will want you to perform . . . to perform . . . um . . . er . . .'

FELICITY: In the village hall.

PAM: In the village hall, for the pantomime, yes. But aside from that. Even when she was helping me into my wedding dress, what she said was, 'Well dear, all I can tell you is to grasp . . . grasp . . .'

FELICITY: The nettle.

PAM: The nettle. Yes. They were terrified to say the words. When I walked down the aisle that day I had no idea what was going to . . . what was going to . . .

FELICITY: Ensue.

PAM: And after it *had* ensued, whether it had been the norm . . .

FELICITY: Your husband, Norm.

PAM: What? No. Normal, what was normal. And the upshot of it all was: I had our son, our first little son, Colin. I was sat up there in the hospital and I had ABSOLUTELY NO IDEA what had caused it.

FELICITY: Oh Pam, that's really sad.

PAM: I know. It *was* sad.

FELICITY: Pam . . .?

PAM: Yes?

FELICITY: What *did* cause it?

The Young Lady of Dorking

There was a young lady of Dorking,
Who when bicycling looked simply corking,
But she had a bad cough
And sadly fell off,
So now she is hawking and walking.

Well Woman Check

I received a notification from my doctor's surgery saying I should attend for a well woman check. My first instinct was to ignore it, but then I told myself that was really stupid. If I didn't look after myself, who would? With resignation and not looking forward to it at all, I rang up and made the appointment.

When I arrived, I realised it must be a clinic, as a lot of women of my sort of age were being processed at the same time. Also, I think you can tell if someone is there for a well woman check because when she is called into the treatment room, she gets up from her chair and walks out of the waiting area with a certain spring in her step, a certain buoyancy, but when she reappears this has mysteriously vanished.

My turn came and I went in. A nurse was carrying out the actual checks.

'Good afternoon, Mrs Russell, if I could ask you to just step on the scales . . .' she said brightly.

I did. There was a pause. She said, 'Now you know, Mrs Russell, that you are overweight?'

I did know but I feigned surprise. 'Am I?' I said.

'Yes, you are.'

I said, 'But I thought I was about the right weight for my height.'

'Well yes,' she replied briskly, 'that would certainly be the case if you were eight feet tall, but as it is, you are *substantially* overweight.'

I blustered a bit, but I knew it was true. If you've put on a few pounds you don't need anybody to tell you, do you? You know yourself, your clothes aren't comfortable any more. Your trouser-legs don't slip up and down, they *grip*. You notice little signs, like when you get into the bath. There doesn't seem to be as much room for the water as there used to be, and you find yourself looking round for somewhere to damp the flannel.

I've got a lot of joke books at home that I've accumulated over the years. Perhaps it says something dubious about us that huge sections of such books are devoted to the subject of people being overweight. All the old chestnuts are in there: 'She was so overweight that she bought a housecoat and it fitted the house.' Or 'He had so many double chins, it was like talking to somebody over a stack of pancakes.'

I have been overweight before, particularly after I had our

two sons, and I didn't like it. The shops never seemed to have anything to fit me and I remember feeling dejected and left out.

This poem is about a young woman who wants to be a model. Indeed she yearns to be a model but unfortunately, she is too fat. You can laugh or cry at this – either is acceptable.

Too Fat

In dreams I prance where models dance and Kate Moss is my
    crony,
And I am thin and nimble like a stick of macaroni,
All the model agencies they clamour for my name,
But there is an obstruction on my path to global fame:
For I'm too fat. Too fat.
I'm round where I was flat,
My trousers used to fit with ease,
Now they don't go past my knees,
My legs are like the trunks of trees,
I'm too fat.

Surgically Enhanced

But I can smell success in great intoxicating whiffs,
I want to be with Naomi where Claudia Sniffer . . . sniffs,
To mince along the catwalk but the people gasp, 'Who's that?
Who can she be, so visibly, so risibly . . . fat!
You're too fat! Too fat!
You're not *modelling* that!
Those massive thighs, those quivering hips!
Those poor defenceless straining zips,
The bum that sank a thousand ships!
You're too fat!'

I used to love the swimming pool, I used to dive and frolic,
Before I heard the filthy words, glutton, chocaholic,
But now upon the diving board I hear the timbers groan,
And skinny women laughing as I stand there on my own,
They say, 'Too fat! Too fat! How do you get like *that*!'
Ridiculed I am, and stung,
I loved those flumes when I was young,
But nowadays I'd be the bung,
I'm too fat.

I've got the diet books, the step, the weights, as you can see,
All the workout tips advised by each celebrity,
I bought a slimmer's wheel, you had to push it to and fro,
But I've pulled so many muscles that it's going to have to go,
'Cause I'm too fat, too fat,
I've bought a load of tat,
Books to help you win the fight,
Pills to blunt your appetite,
Bats to beat your cellulite,
I'm too fat.

I went off to the seaside but I shan't go there again,
Although the day was glorious without a hint of rain,
In my bathing suit I settled back and closed my eyes,
But soon I was awakened by these panic-stricken cries
Of: 'Too fat! Too fat! Don't go near to that!
Call the coastguard!' Voices screech,
'A whale is washed up on the beach!
Roll it back far out of reach!
Too fat!'

This city life begins to pall: the noise, the ceaseless banter,
I hired a horse from a riding school, some mossy path to
    canter,
They led him from the stable, he was saddled up and shod,
He turned his noble head to me and whispered, 'Oh my God!
You're too fat! Too fat!
I'm not carrying that!
You're not getting on my back,
My vertebrae would all go "crack!"
You'd give a horse a heart attack,
You're too fat!'

So I'm going home defeated and I'll lie on my settee,
Away from criticism and from public scrutiny,
I'll have a Walnut Whip because I feel so low today,
Turn up the television so I can't hear people say:
'Too fat! Too fat!
Get a load of that!
She's an armful I'll be bound,
When she walks she shakes the ground,
You don't get many of those to the pound . . .'
I'm too fat.

Punch and Judy Man

I once presented a television show about Weymouth. The idea was that a few people were invited to choose a town that meant something to them, and then present a programme illustrating why. I chose Weymouth because we went there as a family for our first day-trips to the seaside. As children we spent hours unwittingly collecting shells in which the luckless occupant still lived, thus explaining the searing stench which developed when we got them home. We watched with breathless excitement as the holes we dug in the sand filled up with water *on their own*! We jumped the waves. We did what kids do.

I also felt interested in Weymouth because my dad was stationed there in the war. On our day-trips he would go off to the little harbour and look at it thoughtfully. He was there when it teemed with young American servicemen brought over for the D-Day landings, when it was choked with landing craft and preoccupied with the business of war.

He told us interesting stories. He said that along Chesil Beach during the war, he and other soldiers had built structures made of corrugated iron and lengths of pipe. These were supposed to look like guns from the air because we couldn't afford real ones. He said that one day he was strafed by a Messerschmitt and only dived for cover just in time. He conjured up dramatic pictures.

In the programme we also looked at other aspects of the town. Seaside landladies, oyster farming, donkey rides and sure enough, how could we leave it out, the traditional red-and-white-striped, frilly-canopied, flapping-in-the-wind Punch and Judy show.

I was allowed to handle the puppets, peering into the flat white face of the much-thrashed Mrs Punch and the hinged clattering jaws of the crocodile, soon to close on her skinny baby. Nose to nose I inspected the grotesque features and blood-red nightcap of Mr Punch. What a bunch! I handled them with caution as if they might cast some malevolent spell on me.

It was hot that day by the Punch and Judy show. Insufferably hot, with a dry wind coming off the sea. The Punch and Judy Man solicitously enquired as to whether I would like to have a go with Mr Punch. I was not keen to have a go at all, but anxious not to offend, I probed up him with a reluctant finger.

Inside was a rigid tube from which the Punch and Judy man had just withdrawn. It was warm and repulsively sweaty. I put two further fingers into the arms of Mr Punch's frill-necked frock, did a perfunctory nod or two and slid out of him with relief, desperate to wash the digits. I'm not a fan, I'm afraid. Give me the Famous Five any day.

The Pig Epistle
(A psalm-like chant)

And lo I saw before me the birds of the air and the beasts of
all the field,
One among them stood forth, raised up his noble head and
squealed,
He hath a great round nose, his skin all clad in bristle,
And so to the everlasting glory of the pig I give you this . . .
epistle.

The pig hath a wondrous song, hearken to the grunting and
the snort,
And in past times the catching of the greasy pig provided the
youth of the village with much lively sport,
Although the length of time they could hang on to it was not
likely to be long,
And the fragrance left on those that tried was overwhelming
strong.

She walks with a delicate step and mighty swinging of the
udder,
Those of a delicate sensibility may turn up their nose and
shudder,
But while other species never produce offspring that number
as much as four,
The fertile and fecund sow regularly whips out a dozen or
more.

If someone offers you a sheep you must decline with thanks,
For verily the sheep she is as thick as two short planks,
Horses I have never liked, my uncle was to blame,
One kicked him in the teeth and then his smile was never the
    same.

In the name of the sow, the boar, the piglet, hog and swine,
Placed evermore upon this Earth to flourish and to shine,
Hosanna to the pig, so noble and glorious in every fibre,
His brethren shall populate the Earth from here to up the
    Khyber.

As a lifelong friend and confidante, it sure is hard to beat it,
And yet when hardship strikes it's tough, but you can take a
    knife and fork and eat it,
When everyone is out to get you and your troubles seem awful
    big,
Remember that stoutly in the backyard stands a loyal friend,
    his face all covered in swill, remember the piiiiiiiiiiiiiiiiiiiiig.

Wingit

One day I went up the field to feed my chickens. As I approached the run my heart sank. Blowing across the grass and plastered up against the wire netting were great drifts of feathers. 'Oh God,' I thought, 'we've had a visit from the fox. When I open that chicken-house it's going to be carnage in there.'

I approached with a heavy heart, took a deep breath and opened the door, expecting to see blood and feathers. Instead, all six hens strolled casually out and started to feed and scratch about. I was mystified and could not make sense of the scene.

It was not until about a week later that it all fell into place. I was back up there watching the birds, when suddenly one turned side-on to me. Where she should have had a wing there was a ghastly black socket with thin bones protruding like sticks. Her wing had been pulled off. My birds had made themselves a dust bath in a dish-shaped hollow close to the wire, and the fox must have caught her through the fence. It didn't bear thinking about. She'd been left like it for a week.

I rang my sister Jean who keeps a lot of poultry, and asked her what to do. She said, 'I wouldn't hesitate, I'd take her straight to the vet.' I thought, 'Yes, the poor thing's suffered all this week through my lack of observation, it's the least I can do.' I didn't have anything to put her in so I took her in a picnic hamper.

In the vet's surgery there were a collection of people with dogs on leads, cats in those half-moon baskets, hamsters, gerbils, etc. I sat stony-faced because I didn't want anyone to ask me what I had in my basket. If they knew it was a chicken they might have thought I was a twerp.

Eventually I was called in to the treatment room and I put the hamper on the vet's white table. 'It's a chicken,' I said. The vet's face assumed that deliberately blank expression people acquire when they fear they may be dealing with somebody unstable.

'I see,' he said.

I lifted her out and showed her to him. He exclaimed, 'Oh good Lord, what happened?'

I explained.

'Well,' he said, 'I'll do what I can.' He showed me the grim blackening flesh around the wound and went on, 'I'll amputate what's left of the wing and tidy her up a bit, but I'll have to give her a whiff of happy gas. Remember that birds don't cope too well with gas so you mustn't be too optimistic. Ring the surgery at about two and we'll let you know what happened.'

I went home with my empty picnic hamper. At about two o'clock I rang and the receptionist sounded very buoyant. 'Your chicken's come round!' she told me. 'She's sitting up and taking a little wheat, you can come and pick her up.'

When I collected her she was transformed, all smartly stitched up with dissolving sutures and sprayed importantly with purple antiseptic spray. The old girl looked alert and ready for action.

At home I hesitantly put her back with the other hens because the vet said they might peck and bully her. They didn't, she caused not a ripple. All six pottered off.

I was pleased about Wingit, as we all started to call her. Although it was a grisly story, it had a perverse kind of happy ending. The fox got some of her but not all, and she lived to lay another day.

The only thing I don't want you to ask me, is how much money I had to pay the vet. I am much too embarrassed to tell you; but he is driving a new Mercedes.

Voice from the Doomed Dome

I'm the Body in the Body Zone at Greenwich,
Sitting here despondent in the Dome,
My heart is in my boots,
For our work has borne no fruits,
And the visitors we need have stayed at home.

Everyone is very disappointed,
The hordes that we were promised never came,
The sponsors may desert it,
Boots and L'Oréal (I'm worth it),
But no one seems prepared to take the blame.

Surgically Enhanced

Oh won't you come and visit me at Greenwich?
Come by bike or train or tube or boat,
I'll be so glad you did,
We need fifty million quid,
And I know you'd like to help us stay afloat.

We have the best performers here in Greenwich,
See them in our great Millennium Show,
They fly above my head,
Though their audience has fled,
They're so far up I wonder if they *know*.

I'm having such a mean time here in Greenwich,
It's freezing sitting naked on the floor,
Half a woman, half a man,
Half of such a dismal plan,
We're a different kind of body that's for sure.

I don't look like anybody's body!
You wouldn't recognise me as your own,
But you'll know us when you've seen us,
We have just one arm between us,
And my polystyrene heart has turned to stone.

This used to be a scene of dereliction,
Redundancy, finality, decay,
Buildings no one heeded,
Or cared about, or needed,
Similar to what we have today.

I feel the clammy hand of dismal failure,
Helplessly we drift towards the drop,

We have just one final chance,
As a bloke from Disney, France,
Has come across to save us from the chop.

Soon they'll be disposing of the Body,
Disposing of a Body not required,
What a waste of all my charm,
My two heads and single arm,
Of the Body, in the Body Zone. (Expired)

Automatic Telephone Answering Systems

With the onslaught of crabby old age, I find that certain things annoy me more than they used to. I was always fairly placid but these days if things make me ratty, I don't necessarily feel I should keep quiet about it.

A good example would be hot-air hand driers in toilets. What a joke and an irritant. I watch women in toilets. I don't want you to misconstrue that, of course, but I do. The average woman emerges from the cubicle, washes her hands briskly, then looks round hopefully for a dispenser of paper towels. Dream on, sister. Unless you're in a rare enlightened establishment, what you're provided with is a hot-air hand drier. You stick your hands under the meekly puffing grille and wait a fortnight for perfect rasping dryness. In almost all cases the woman gives up and leaves while wiping her dripping hands on her clothing or, as in my case, her hair. Yes, yes, I know it's probably greener not to produce that paper waste. It's just that the alternative method is ineffectual. It doesn't work.

Another modern innovation which makes me boil with rage is the automatic telephone answering system. I like to talk to a person. If I have a problem I'd like to discuss it with someone friendly on the other end of the phone and resolve it. Well, you can't. Nowadays you can't. Instead you have to listen to a recorded voice offering you alternatives. You hear the options and press the relevant button. If you want such-and-such, press hash. I don't know what hash is. Corned beef hash. Hash browns. You press hash.

Now you are filtered into what you hope is the right department. You'd love to speak to a human being but alas, you hear only another recorded voice which informs you:

'All our operators are busy at the moment. Your call is important to us. You are currently number forty-six in the queue . . .'

Now comes the blood-boiler. They play you recorded music. You rage because you do not want to listen to music, you do not know how long you are going to have to listen to music for, and certainly you do not want to *pay* to listen to the music, which you are probably having to do. In my case I find the recording is usually of Vanessa-Mae playing *The Four Seasons* on her electric violin. By this time, and I know it's not very Christian, I wouldn't mind if Vanessa Mae was electrocuted *by* her electric violin if I could only stop wasting my time and *talk to somebody*!

I have started to write a protest poem. Being deeply stressful to do, this is all I have produced so far:

If you would like to meet the person who installed this
    automatic telephone answering system, and shoot him with
    a *gun*,
Press *one*.

Devastated

Empty-handed at the last we're devastated,
All these weary years that we have waited,
Now Uncle's quit the scene,
And we never got a bean,
And in our hour of grief we are prostrated.

He biked along the cliff, exhilarated,
The wind was in his hair, he was elated,
Then Uncle scribed an arc,
And for him the world went dark,
And his false teeth bit the sand and masticated.

Surgically Enhanced

In truth his poor old brakes were antiquated,
In gin his poor old brain was marinated,
He thought that he could stop,
But he never saw the drop,
And now before his loved ones he is crated.

With fittings made of brass it's decorated,
Fastened down with rivets bifurcated,
His cat is in despair,
Caterwauling everywhere,
But it's done that ever since it was castrated.

We went to see the lawyer aforestated,
Who by the word of law was regulated,
He read to us the will,
And gave to us the bill,
And wouldn't take a cheque that was post-dated.

So to a life of scrimping we are fated,
Our semi now will never be updated,
We'd better start to save,
To get a microwave,
Empty-handed at the last we're devastated.

On the Panama Canal

Sometimes I perform my one-woman show on one of the big cruise ships. I like cruising, where you unpack your suitcase once into a cosy cabin, then sit back and let the sights of the world come to you. It's comforting, to a worrier like me, that while you are adventurously exploring foreign parts, the ship sits waiting for you in the bay like a large fond mummy. Also, on a cruising holiday I go home with most of my belongings, having not left them littered behind me in various hotel rooms.

Once I was working on the P&O ship *Oriana* as it went through the Panama Canal and up to Acapulco and San Francisco. It was fascinating to see the canal. I remember being taught about it in the primary school in Stanford-in-the-Vale, seeing photographs and being told what a phenomenal achievement it was, what a marvellous feat of engineering. Half a century later I was thrilled to think I was actually going to travel through the canal.

The ship carried a lady lecturer who gave lively talks about interesting points along the journey and the next port of call. I always went along to them because I think the more you know about a place, the more you get out of actually seeing it.

During the talk I was pleased to hear that along the banks of the Panama Canal, in the humid conditions that prevailed, it was quite possible that we'd see wild alligators basking in the sun. I'm very interested in wildlife and had never seen a wild alligator. I knew what to look for because I've seen my granny's handbag, but I'd never seen them wild in their own habitat. I was quite excited.

The Panama Canal is entered through a series of monumental locks called the Gatun Locks. These look like the locks you see along our rivers and canals except that they are on a vast scale, to cope with enormous ships.

We approached the Gatun Locks and inched into the massive lock chamber. Our great polished white ship towered above the buildings and baking-hot quayside. Alongside us was a container ship, an old rust-bucket of a craft called the *Kenwood*. I kept looking at it to see if it had whipped up a Victoria sandwich, but it hadn't.

Anyway, I commandeered a spot up on deck by the ship's rail early, because I wanted to get a close look at the alligators. Therefore I was leaning on the rail, idly looking at the activity on the *Kenwood*, when the smaller ship suddenly let out a great hoot from its hooter just below where I was standing. It wasn't like a *Carry On* film, I didn't exactly turn round with a soot-blackened face, but it did propel into the air a cloud of black smuts, and one lodged in my eye.

I didn't worry about it at first, I just did what you do to try to get things out of your eye. I dabbed it with my handkerchief, my husband dabbed it with his, but we couldn't shift it. After a while my eye became inflamed and streamed with tears. There was something sharp under the eyelid and every time I blinked I could feel it scratch my eyeball.

The ship progressed along the canal and soon the alligators came into view. People ran from side to side. There were excited shouts: 'Look at that one! It's massive! Look, there's a family group! Look! This is fantastic!'

I could hear all this going on, but to my disgust and acute disappointment I was down in the ship's medical centre waiting to get my eye treated. I couldn't believe it. What timing! I was irritated, crabby, and *narked*. I felt like this right up until the moment when I was shown into the surgery and saw the doctor.

Now that doctor, I have to tell you, was one of the most devastatingly handsome men I have ever seen. All thoughts of alligators went out of my head. He stood up as I entered. He was tall, slim, broad-shouldered and reminiscent of a young Sean Connery with glossy dark hair and beautiful brown eyes like chocolate drops. Deeply suntanned, he was dressed from head to foot in white naval uniform with epaulettes bearing the medical insignia in red, black and gold.

I could have put my husband out with the rubbish.

I expect he was equally impressed to see me, as I scrutinised him with one eye. I explained what had happened and he invited me to lie on the bed. I couldn't get up there quick enough. He came forward and examined my eye.

Whenever I go to the optician to have my eyes examined I always find certain parts of the procedure embarrassing. In particular, that moment when they come at you with a little pointed light, and they move it up, down and side to side, with their face so close to yours that you can feel their breath on your skin. It's such an intimate situation yet with a complete stranger. Well, I hate that. As a rule I hate that. Yet on this occasion for some reason, I didn't seem to mind at all.

He had a good look at my eye and he said in his beautiful rich resonant voice:

'Oh yes. I can see what the problem is. I can see that you have a sharp particle embedded beneath your upper eyelid and, if you are agreeable, I would recommend a simple, painless medical procedure: that I introduce a saline wash.'

I said, 'I'm agreeable, Doctor. *I am agreeable*. You can introduce anything you like.'

So he removed it. I spent the rest of the journey through the Panama Canal up on deck trying to get a smut in my other eye, but I didn't have any luck.

Holiday Afloat

We're on the *Oriana*, she's so beautiful and strong,
Her décor so exquisite and her corridors . . . so long,
I feel a grand excitement as the band begins to play,
She turns to face the sea, casts off her ropes and sails away.

We cruise on *Oriana* where, with luxury and ease,
We slip between the continents across the seven seas,
We're sailing for America upon a western track,
And I haven't got a clue which is the front and which the back.

The motion of the vessel and the rolling of the sea,
The moon upon the ocean's like a Paradise to me,
The curving of the planet and the passage of the sun,
The terrifying toilet where you press the switch and *run*!

We had a little fracas when unpacking all our clothes,
The woman needs the hanging space – everybody knows!
But all is now resolved and there is harmony once more,
I've got thirty hangers and he's settled for a drawer.

But oh! That force eleven! Fifteen-metre swells and more!
The teacups and the crockery that shot across the floor,
Seasick in my cabin I was helpless, I was weak,
My wardrobe may be little but by God it can't half creak.

The choices of activity are staggering at sea,
Bridge, keep fit or handicrafts, which are the ones for me?
Or if you're tired of living, give the laundrette a blast,
Take somebody's washing out and see how long you last.

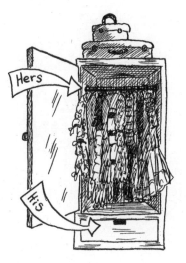

I wrote this on board the *Oriana* and we sold it in aid of the RNLI; it raised £5,000!

Inland Waterways

Now and then, as I toil along motorways or shoot through the countryside on a packed train, I look out and catch a glimpse of a canal. Just for a second I see a winding waterway of exactly the right width, and the pleasing curves of a small white bridge. There might be a lock-keeper's picturesque house, the garden bright with flowers, and massive black-and-white timber lock gates set in mown grass. Everywhere there would be smartly painted narrow boats moored companionably nose to tail, or bustling off to some enticing and beautiful waterway pub.

I always view these scenes with regret and a sense of loss. They seem to say, 'Look how lovely we are and you never come near us! You never even look twice.'

I want to say, 'I do! I will! One day I'll get out of this stale, suffocating train and I'll sail down that cool green water. I'll slip under the darling bridge, those descending branches will envelop me and I'll be gone, just swallowed up into the scene and gone . . .'

One day I finally had the chance of a long weekend on the Kennet and Avon Canal. When I excitedly told my best friend, her response was meagre and dampening. She said she had boarded a narrow boat with her husband and two children for a similar holiday. They had set off in high spirits. After they had travelled slowly in the rain for the entire morning, the offspring became bored. Having raked over and consumed most of the food, they now squabbled and complained about the slowness of the journey. Husband and wife fell out. My friend called up a taxi on her mobile, got off at the next road bridge, and with a sharp 'Bugger this for a lark!' went home and left them to it. I was sure my own holiday would be serene and harmonious, but an unwelcome seed of doubt had been sown.

On the day of the trip my husband and I turned up at the wharf in Devizes with a remarkable amount of baggage, two sons and a black dog. From the wharf shop we bought canal maps, information on waterways etiquette and pamphlets on the wildlife we might glimpse on our travels. I was startled to see goldfish and terrapins listed. Apparently people get fed up with keeping them as pets and dump them in the canal.

Our narrow boat seemed very large and not in the first flush of youth. My husband had never skippered this or any other craft before. We were given a fairly perfunctory account of its workings, then set off in glorious sunshine. All seemed well until another boat appeared coming towards us. My husband blanched. He said, 'It's like driving a cricket pitch!' and as the approaching craft neared he muttered through ashen lips: 'I hope that bloke knows how to avoid me because I sure as hell don't know how to avoid him!' A desperate silence descended on our vessel as the gap narrowed, and we steeled ourselves for the splintering of wood and cries of anguish. The two craft glided silently past each other.

In due course a fragile confidence developed but this evaporated when we saw our first lock. Locks are very dark and frightening. One of your party goes, without conviction, to the lock mechanism and turns it the wrong way. After numerous failures the great black doors yawn open and you sail forward as if into a trap. The doors close. The water-level drops. You lose sight of the sunny banks and descend into the pit. Shaggy, streaming black walls loom over you like those of a tomb or foul dungeon. Curious faces peer down from the rim. For those onlookers you pathetically endeavour to look seasoned and confident. The descent ceases and suddenly the black doors part, relief floods in and the sunlit waterway stretches ahead. The ordeal is over and you sail out and away.

Our dog Gemma came from a dogs' home. She was anxious to please but unsure about sailing. Mortified at the prospect of jumping on and off the boat, she only did so after much loud encouragement, in an eyes-shut 'Well if I *must*' fashion, which meant she usually fell in. We had to keep fishing her out. Nervous and looking for reassurance, she took to creeping alongside our beds in the dead of night and, finding any drooping human hands, set about them with great wet slapping licks. People were galvanised with terror and sat bolt upright in the cramped cabins, cracking their heads. We thought a serpent had risen up from the silt.

I liked being on the canal but did not enjoy the cooking. The fresh air gave my family voracious appetites. No sooner had I produced one meal and washed up awkwardly in the miniature sink than they were enquiring about the next. It was blazingly hot and conditions in the tiny kitchen became stifling and ratty.

One evening I was cooking an intricate and complicated dish, a pan of sausages. There were too many for the small frying pan and they rose up the sides. I had to keep stirring them so that they all obtained a fleeting glimpse of the heat. It was boiling hot, poised above the spitting pan, but upon opening the little sliding window before me I was blinded by a cloud of mosquitoes which swarmed in, fangs first, looking for blood. On we sailed with the chef sweating and swatting. After that night we took to eating in pubs.

I also learned to do the narrow-boat walk. The layout of many boats seems to consist of a long corridor up the right-hand side with the little rooms giving off to the left. Therefore the wall to your right becomes the curving ceiling over your head and if you are tall and walk normally, you scrape your shoulder and crack your head. This calls for the narrow-boat walk, whereby from the feet to the pelvis the body faces forwards and from waist to neck it turns sideways, with the head also facing forwards to see where you are going. It takes a bit of practice.

Certainly the trip awakened my latent resourcefulness. Our son James celebrated his birthday on the second day out. Having forgotten to bring Sellotape, I fixed the jolly giftwrap around his presents with dental floss.

To make the birthday special, we had a secret plan. We would potter along the canal, not letting on that all had been set up in advance, and exclaim, 'Why, here's a cracking-looking village. Let's go and see if there's anywhere nice to eat!' Amazingly we would then happen upon an exquisite thatched inn (previously picked from a waterway pub guide) and upon entering find a table set up with birthday balloons, cake etc. It was a grand plan to fill any fond parent's heart with anticipation. The only trouble was the slowness of the boat.

The morning's leisurely pace quickened towards the afternoon. Conspiratorial smiles on parental faces froze as the clock spun. By teatime we were flat out at four miles an hour, the breeze stirring my husband's hair as he urged the great lumbering oaf of a boat forward. Consulting the map, we found we were still *miles* from the village. Panic set in. We rang the pub at seven, eight and nine o'clock to say we were running late, and only finally sprinted in, crazed with hunger, at ten o'clock. To the landlord's everlasting credit, even at that late hour the birthday supper was ready and welcoming. I learned that on the canals you have to allow *plenty* of time for your journey.

I Love a Little Narrow Boat

I love a little narrow boat, I love the old canal,
Imagining the tales these ancient waterways could tell,
I love to work the locks, those oaken gates so firm and
    strong,
With know-alls up above to tell you what you're doing wrong.

I love to see the native creatures busy at the brink,
The otter and the water vole, the terrapin and mink,
And peering in the water, into shallows green and still,
To see somebody's goldfish from the kitchen window-sill.

I love to moor along the bank and hear the gentle rain,
To cook a meal and watch the world beyond the window-
    pane,
Little bobbing moorhen chicks, the mallard and the coot,
Exhausted lovers hoping that their effort's bearing fruit.

I love the ancient bridges, every keystone, every corbel,
The singing of the little birds, the chirrup and the warble,
To feed a lonely swan, so perfect, white as alabaster,
Who struck me with his wing; observe my collar-bone in
    plaster.

I love to meet the other folk who use the waterways,
The walkers and the fishermen on sunny languid days,

We drift beside the towpath and we breathe the summer's
    breath,
Till roaring motor-bikers come and frighten us to death.

I love the inland waterways and if it's in my power,
I'll just keep on a-sailing at about three miles an hour,
And when I see that final tunnel, into it I'll glide,
I'll raise my yachting cap and see you on the other side.

Global Warming

Global warming, unheard-of a decade ago but horribly familiar to us all now. It sounds like a huge subject, one that concerns cataclysmic happenings: holes in the ozone layer and continent-sized icebergs bearing down upon us. Massive issues. Too enormous for non-scholars to understand, in fact. Little did I know that global warming was going to descend on my little speck of Gloucestershire and affect me. That it would appear and interfere with the workings of my wood-burning stove.

I love my wood-burning stove. It's a big, black, warm, comforting presence, safe and homely. You can put any old wood on it and no matter how much it might spit and fume, no flaming brands can shoot out to burn a great smoking hole in your carpet, or startle the sleeping dog.

We had it installed ourselves. In the hall, when we first came to live in our house, there was a wide, generous fireplace filled in with a sheet of hardboard upon which had been screwed a mean two-bar electric fire in a shade of aqua. We decided to take all that out and install a wood burner. We consulted our builder, a venerable gent as old as time itself. We asked him what needed to be done.

'Line the chimley,' he ordered in a voice from the crypt. 'Be sure to line the chimley, 'cause if you don't, arter a time, runnin' all down the inside of the brickwork, you'll get rivers of treacle.' *Rivers of treacle!* I could feel the hairs standing up on the back of my neck. A river of treacle! We agreed to have the chimney lined and in due course a silver spiral was wrestled into our house and thrust up the flue.

Granted the timing was bad. Our stove has glass windows through which the flickering flames are only visible for the first twenty minutes. After that, rock-hard crusted deposits build up, which have to be scraped off by a blackened operative, usually myself. Only weeks after we bought our stove, an advanced version was introduced which fanned currents of hot air down over the inner windows, keeping them crystal clear. Anyway, that having been said, ours worked well.

Years passed. The stove did a fine job, squat and hot in the hall. Then last Christmas a noxious smell began to be detectable in the area. It thickened and crept upstairs to the bedrooms. A rank stench of soot and hellish tar floated into all parts of the house. It was disgusting, like a battalion of laughing chain-smokers. Filled with foreboding I went to investigate. Peering over the crouching back of the cold wood-burning stove I could see the thing of my nightmares. Coiled on the stone flags lay *a river of treacle*! It was black and viscous. It stank. The owner of the voice from the crypt having long since gone before, I called out another expert.

This one was short, with a penetrating stare. 'It's global warmin',' he said.

'What?' I asked, incredulous.

'It's global warmin'. The rain's not coming vertical any more, it's coming *horizontal*.'

'Really?' I asked, fairly sceptical.

'Yep, it's going straight under yer baffle, down into yer soot trap and now yer soot trap's leaked. That's what all this black is. Yer soot trap's rusted through.'

'Oh my God,' I said. 'Me soot trap! Can it be mended?'

Indeed it could. Quick as a flash he shinned up the ladder, put a thing like an upturned casserole on the chimney and charged me a hundred and fifty quid.

It's amazing how global warming is affecting us all.

Global Warming

The poor old planet's on its knees,
I fear I've over-fished the seas,
It's all my fault and serve me right,
For eating fish on Friday night.

My homely fire of glowing coals,
Has helped to melt the icy poles,
I dread to see when next I look,
An iceberg floating up the brook.

Surgically Enhanced

Geraniums out in their pot,
Have all collapsed, it's far too hot,
Approach the hose we never can,
We're frightened of the hosepipe ban.

The reservoirs have all run dry,
No rain clouds fleck the clear blue sky,
It's global warming spit or bust,
My old front lawn has turned to dust.

I'll try to act a bit more green,
And shift my bonfire from the scene,
Nor laugh to see my neighbour choke,
As his garden fills with smoke.

I will not fling upon the fires,
Mattresses and old car tyres,
To finer feelings I shall yield,
I'll tip them in the farmer's field.

For fifteen years this push-bike lay,
And never saw the light of day,
I've dragged it out into the sun,
And covered it in 3-IN-ONE.

Now off recycling I shall ride,
To feed the daleks side by side,
With textiles, paper, glass and leather,
Shoes in pairs and tied together.

Here's a bank I seem to know,
With bristly holes where bottles go,

I push them in, the browns and greens,
And hear them smash to smithereens.

Consider this recycling yard,
Look at all that we discard:
Anything compostable,
And lonely women on the pull.

Gas guzzling cars, they make me boil,
We're powered by sunflower oil!
And thus our car on normal trips,
Emits the smell of fish and chips.

Too much water, it was clear,
Our family was wasting here,
To rectify it I was quick,
And in the cistern put a brick.

Our energy comes from the sun,
With solar panels by the ton,
So heavy did the blighters grow,
Our house is now a bungalow.

I'm dolphin friendly, GM free,
Low emission, green, PC,
Organic, fresh, free range and pure,
But my husband's gone to live next door.

Woodland Burial

Don't lay me in some gloomy churchyard shaded by a wall,
Where the dust of ancient bones has spread a dryness over all,
Lay me in some leafy loam where, sheltered from the cold,
Little seeds investigate, and tender leaves unfold
There, kindly and affectionately plant a native tree
To grow resplendent before God and hold some part of me.
The roots will not disturb me as they wend their peaceful way
To build the fine and bountiful from closure and decay,
To seek their small requirements so that when their work is
    done
I'll be tall and standing strongly in the beauty of the sun.

Crabby Christmas

I've got my own Nativity set, with figures carved from wood,
I put it on the sideboard every year, it looks quite good,
Mary's dressed in blue, see there's a little seat for her,
And a crib for baby Jesus with his frankincense and myrrh.

Now I fully understand that all good things come to an end,
And I must scrap my little set for fear it may offend
All the Hindus, Buddhists, Muslims, Trappists, Sikhs, well, all
   the flock,
Who might see my baby Jesus and be paralysed with shock.

Forget the Christmas dinner as my appetite is small
For a poor old shut-up turkey which has had no life at all;
They are created creatures though their plight we cannot see,
And though they may be cheap they don't look bootiful to me.

Hear the rasping of the tinsel and the rattle of the cash,
The streets are full of shoppers and the shops are full of trash,
Christmas is a-comin', tally-ho and toodle-oo,
There's a Santa on the chimney and his leg is down the flue.

There's a reindeer on the rooftop, there are sleigh-bells on the
    sled,
There is flickering and flashing, and they're going white and
    red,
The silent starry night is by illumination rent,
I know God said 'I am the light' but is this what he meant?

See my neighbour's house: there's an electric yuletide log,
A robin and a snowman and a yes! Kermit the frog,
The local power station it is standing all aglow,
And it's heading for a meltdown like Chernobyl long ago.

I am going down the garden, I am going down the shed,
If anybody wants me you can tell them I have fled.
I might emerge on Boxing Day if common sense prevails,
And I'll buy you all a present, they'll be cheaper in the sales.

Don't Bother, I'll Do It Myself

(On bringing up teenagers)

Now I've had his report saying 'Just the right sort!
Motivated; a jolly good show!
He's keen, energetic, determined, athletic!'
Well, where is he? Where did he go?

Could this sleeper, this blob, help with one little job?
And exhibit some vigour and health?
I would wake him and ask, it's too much of a task,
So don't bother, I'll do it myself.

Surgically Enhanced

In his bedroom I stand with the Pledge in my hand,
And it's tricky to know where to start,
But one thing's for sure, that I can't see the floor,
The place has been taken apart!

Buying food, off I dash, and the plastic I flash,
Round the vast supermarket I fly,
I was straight when I went, but I finish up bent
By the weight of the shopping I buy.

I have lost all my charms, grown orang-utan arms,
As I lope along clearing each shelf,
So it would have been great if you'd washed up your plate,
But don't bother, I'll do it myself!

On White Horse Hill

I want to go where harebells blow,
Where birds of prey are soaring,
To stand my ground on the Castle Mound,
When winter winds are roaring.

To steal and creep to the Dingles deep,
With cress and mosses growing,
And lie at ease on fallen trees,
Where sweetest springs are flowing.

The fall and sweep of the Manger steep,
Short grass the sheep have nibbled,
To feel the chill on Dragons Hill,
See where the blood has dribbled!

Explore the myth of Wayland Smith,
Where in some magic manner,
An ancient force will take my horse,
And shoe him for a tanner.

This Vale is mine, its names divine,
From Kingston Lyle to Goosey,
I learned them all when I was small,
From Shellingford to Pusey.

But Uffington, ah, she's the one,
The chalk and thatch and steeple,
Bill and George at Packer's Forge,
My own familiar people.

But in these times of rougher rhymes,
John Betjeman's work alluring,
Is like the beauty of the Vale,
Sharp, timeless and enduring.

(For the unveiling of the blue plaque on Sir John Betjeman's former home
at Uffington, 24 June 2006.)

Unfed Calf

Steve Poole stuck his fingers in the calf's mouth,
'If the suck reflex has gone,' he said, 'we've had it.'
I picked up the calf, heavy, a dead still weight,
And ran for the little stable and confining yard.
Min ran behind, gross untapped udder thumping from side to
    side,
Brown face frantic with concern, moaning with maternity,
The arch villain,
The bad mother.

Min, distracted by a bucket of nuts.
The calf is trundled forward, nose first, jammed in position
    with a knee at the back,

Surgically Enhanced

'Now then, Titch,' says Steve Poole, clasping the muzzle, 'now
   then, get in there.'
Whack! A great ratty hoof swings forward.
Thwack! in the surprised face of the hungry calf
who retires defeated.
Perhaps not, then.
Perhaps I'll just stay hungry then.

Back in position. Careful transference of the hopeful sucking,
The ridged palate, from barren finger to fruitful teat.
Min munches the nuts.
We hold still and watch the calf,
See the sweet beautiful undulations of the throat as it swallows,
The curve of the neck. The shock of interest.
At last a flow of relieving colostrum,
The lifesaver.

Good girl, Min, we rub her pin bones. Good girlie, Min.
New life for the calf, rejected and fading,
Now its hollow belly swells roundly out,
Fat with special recipe,
Primrose yellow,
Antibodies,
Anti-baddies,
Mum's magic.

Too Much of a Fag

Observe the poor old smoker,
How sheepishly he stands
Upon the frozen pavement,
A fag cupped in his hands.
His clothes are never fragrant,
His breath is never clean,
He is shunned by his companions
And hooked on nicotine.

See down the blasted alleyway,
Whipped by each rainy gust,
He cowers into doorways,
Inhaling, crazed with lust.
His respiratory system,
If he could just have looked,
Is black as all damnation
And like his goose . . .
Is cooked.

Silver Wedding Speech

On BBC Radio 4, on 5 April 2007, there was a programme called *Never too Late to Separate*. This concerned couples who opted to mark their silver, golden and even longer anniversaries by getting divorced. 'They realise that they have spent years focusing on being parents at the expense of being partners' was one explanation. Put simply, when the kids have gone they look at the other half and think: No.

This programme gave me the idea for 'Silver Wedding Speech'. My poem implies no criticism of my own extremely satisfactory husband. Well, not much anyway.

Silver Wedding Speech

My friends and relations from far destinations,
The sweet homely pals of my youth,
Here to drink a libation at our celebration,
I might as well tell you the truth.
It's our silver, you see, our anniversary,
And I speak from the heart though it's tough,
We've had joy, we've had tears, for twenty-five years,
And twenty-five years is enough.

So take down the marquee, don't erect it for me,
Take the tabletop garlands and fruit,
Have the napkins and wine, I won't stay to fine-dine,
Forgive me but I'm going to shoot.
These twenty years gone, I've been soldiering on,
And over the cracks I have varnished,
But enough is enough and although it sounds rough,
A little like silver you've tarnished.

Twenty-five years ago, as some of you know,
With the ties matrimonial knotted,
It was 'Here comes the bride' while the relatives cried,
Like a little brown shrimp I was potted.
Well that was then, this is now. I'm resigned to a row,
For I know there'll be protests and howls,

But for my sanity's sake, I've had all I can take
Of your prejudices and your bowels.

I've got so much to do. Take a gap year . . . or two!
In however few years are remaining.
I'll be free, free at last, of the chains of the past,
No cooking! Nobody complaining!
And if I fall ill and lie lonely and chill,
I know there'll be no one to care then,
No one comforting me, no nice hot cup of tea,
No attention. Well, nothings changed there then.

Surgically Enhanced

Though the kids loved me once, now I'm old and a dunce,
A codger whose life is behind me.
Great long-suffering sighs and the rolling of eyes
Show how interesting they find me.
I acknowledge, I do, golden times spent with you,
As in the silvery spotlight we bask,
You've a place in my heart but till death us do part
Is just a bit too much to ask.

The Pension Poem

On 14 March 2007, I was sixty years old. One morning shortly before my birthday I opened the post and had a shock . . .

A letter came this morning and it fluttered to the floor,
I picked it up and read, as I've done countless times before.
Well I laughed! I doubled up! I stamped my foot and slapped
    my thigh,
I couldn't get my breath, the tears were streaming from my
    eyes.
I mean, they'd got the right address, they'd even found my
    proper name,
But the heading said 'State Pension – it is time to make your
    claim.'

State Pension! Well I ask you! You know I'm not one to scold,
But this was meant for some old dear, with silver threads
    among the gold,
Some doddering old fogey long ago turned out to grass,
With enormous varifocals and her gnashers in a glass.
Some elderly old personage who shuffles round the shops,
With a little tartan shopping bag and porridge round her
    chops.

Well it's not me, I assure you! Not to whom this claim refers,
I won't be a *pensioner* for ages! Years and years!
My life has hardly started! It's not *finished*, that's for sure!
I've only got two kids . . . well, I might have a couple more!
I have got a sense of humour, but they ought to take more
    care,
Someone in Human Resources needs one up the derrière.

Imagine sending that to me! It must have been a prank,
It's probably my husband, yes, it's him I've got to thank.
I'm not getting old, I'm staying young like Peter Pan,
So don't you 'pension' me like some incontinent old gran.
Take back this application with no further ifs or buts,
And think along the lines of where the monkey puts his nuts.

A pensioner! A pensioner! Well that *would* be a treat,
Imagine my excitement as I sit and soak my feet,
A timorous old biddy with a handrail up the path,
And a ruddy great device to get me in and out the bath.
A pendant round my neck which I just have to press and then
Haring up our stairs come General Custer and his men.

Well that's not me! That is not me! Look, I've kept my
    youthful figure!
These aren't age-spots upon my face, they're freckles . . . only
    bigger!
Not so long ago strong men competed for my honour,
So let's have no more nonsense! I'm a goer, not a gonner!
For ME to be a pensioner, I say with some relief,
I'd be sixty in 07! . . . Wait a minute . . . Oh GOOD GRIEF!

I am Ready, Mr Prescott

I am ready, Mr Prescott. You can take me in your arms,
All these years I've waited to experience your charms,
So fling aside those trousers, I hope they're quick release,
For all that hanky-panky's made you clinically obese.

I like a man of substance, I like a man of size,
Especially when I'm measuring the bags beneath his eyes,
If anyone insulted me, I have no doubt at all,
You'd leap to my defence and punch the blighter through the
    wall.

Oh I like you, Mr Prescott, a constant watch I keep,
To see you on TV sat next to Tony, fast asleep,
So I'm waiting, Mr Prescott, my toothbrush in my bag,
To see your chiselled jaw behind the wheel of either Jag.

A man like you is dangerous, a man like you is trouble,
Just like a row of houses you demolished me to rubble,
With one hand on the tiller, as steady as a rock,
And the other disappearing up the secretary's frock.

Through the Lens

I place it on my finger like a little mixing bowl
Surprisingly, I'm nervous, not entirely in control.
My pulse has started racing and my mouth is going dry
But I'm going to take this contact lens and stick it in my eye!

Well I've got it on my fingertip but riddled now with doubt,
Is the thing the right way up, or back to front or inside out?
And someone always mentions, as you angle it in vain
That it might travel round your eyeball and be never seen again.

My eyelids start to flutter as the shaking finger nears
Protectively they wink and squint and blink away the tears,
Then gah! The day is lost! A spasm flicks it on your lap,
This little bit of polythene, this little crumpled scrap.

And if you lose a lens it's more traumatic than you think,
I've seen frantic people clawing at the plughole of the sink,
People in their underclothes, people in the buff
Crawling round the carpet analysing bits of fluff.

But I won't give up, not if I have to stay here half the night
With my magnifying mirror and enormous blinding light.
You may be queuing for the bathroom, I don't care how much
    time passes,
For when I see you next . . . I'll be the one without the glasses.